Branding Basics for Small Business

How to Create an Irresistible Brand on Any Budget

2nd Edition

Maria Ross

Praise for
Branding Basics for Small Business

Marketing no longer means advertising, and brand no longer means logo. Your brand is the promise, the experience, the interactions, and the expectation people have for you. Maria Ross understands this, and teaches you how to think about this essential element of your business.

Seth Godin
Author of *Meatball Sundae and Linchpin*

....

Maria Ross makes it clear that branding isn't just for big companies, rich companies, or consumer companies. It's for your company. In a single readable volume, she shows you how to separate yourself from the pack and win.

Marty Neumeier
Author of *The Brand Gap, Zag,*
and *Metaskills: Five Talents for the Robotic Age*

....

Match your authentic purpose with the courage to serve only the right customer (not any customer). That's the essence of a successful business you will fall in love with. Maria's book is the recipe for getting there. Dig in!

Mike Michalowicz
Author of *The Toilet Paper Entrepreneur,*
The Pumpkin Plan, and *Profit First*

....

Creating content that captivates customers, differentiates your organization and drives sales is vital today. But the first step is getting crystal-clear on your brand strategy. Before you dive into the tactics to produce random acts of content, read this book!

Ann Handley
Chief Content Officer of MarketingProfs
Co-author of *Content Rules:*
How to Create Killer Blogs, Podcasts, Videos, Ebooks
(and More) that Engage Customers and Ignite Your Business

Maria Ross cuts through the fluff and explains why strong brands are built on customers' experiences and not on huge advertising budgets. Complete with real examples from top companies, this book is a roadmap leading small businesses and entrepreneurs in the right direction.

Adam Sutton
MarketingSherpa.com

....

(This book) is a wise and recommended read, not to be missed by any small business.

Midwest Book Review

....

Such a wide and clear scope on what makes successful brands so—successful. Great coverage. And great inspiration to be true to your values and think big.

Danielle LaPorte
Author of *The Fire Starter Sessions: A Soulful + Practical Guide to Creating Success on Your Own Terms* and *The Desire Map*

....

Any organization looking to be more successful and get to the next level will benefit from the smart insights and fascinating, real-world stories in this book. Building a brand isn't easy, nor is managing an existing brand's reputation—especially in this time of online reviews and social media wildfire. Whether you're trying to figure out what a brand is, thinking about rebranding, or ready to blast your brand full speed ahead, Maria cuts to the chase and tells you everything you need to know. This is invaluable for everyone, especially organizations with limited time and resources that need results–fast."

Whitney Keyes
Professor of strategic communications and global reputation management, Seattle University
Author of *Propel: Five Ways to Amp Up Your Marketing and Accelerate Business*

As someone who has worked with thousands of small businesses, I have seen the lack of a clear, focused brand strategy cause people to waste time, energy, money, and to flounder in the marketplace. Never fear, Maria breaks down branding so that anyone with a business, or who is thinking of launching a business, can understand why an investment in branding is make or break for creating a thriving business. Don't launch without it!

Beth Schoenfeldt
Founder & CEO, FundedBuy

With *Branding Basics for Small Business*, Maria Ross offers a clear + compelling definition of what a "brand" really is: *Your company's reputation, personality, and reason for being—all rolled into one package.* If your "package" is less than phenomenal -- or long overdue for a re-boot -- this book is a little treasure. Dive in.

Alexandra Franzen
Writer, Workshop Leader, and
Author of *50 Ways to Say You're Awesome*

So many small businesses and entrepreneurs are intimidated and overwhelmed by the concept of branding. What is it? Where do I start? What does it even mean? Maria Ross breaks down branding into easy, doable steps and her writing is engaging, fun and jargon-free. This is a must-read for anybody who's struggling with who to market to and how to reach them.

Sarah Von Bargen
Blogger, Writer, and Internet Awesome-ifier
sarahvonbargen.com

Branding Basics for Small Business:
How to Create an Irresistible Brand on Any Budget
(2nd Edition)
Copyright © 2010, 2014 by Maria Ross

NorLightsPress.com
762 State Road 458
Bedford, IN 47421

Printed in the United States of America

ISBN: 978-1-935254-87-4

Cover Design by Bridget Perez, TRAY Creative
Book Design by Nadene Carter
Author Photo by Alison Jensen

Dedication

For Paul.

And for all the entrepreneurs, small businesses, start-ups, and non-profits who bring passion to their work and purpose to their brands. Thank you for being my heroes. The world would be boring without you.

Contents

Introduction

Why Small Business Owners, Entrepreneurs, and Nonprofits Need This Book

EVERY DAY OF OUR LIVES we're forced to endure bad marketing. Today, we humans create and assimilate a barrage of corporate messages and images that was unheard of a century ago. The noise gets louder as companies fight to rise above the crowd. The moment they find a new way to do this, the tactic is abused and destroyed until it breaks down and the next new thing arrives to take its place.

I've had enough. *I want to start a brand revolution.*

I admit it: During my marketing, advertising, and branding career, I've been guilty of adding to the scrap pile on occasion. This was simply because we were not always operating from a strong brand foundation and were just chasing the next new thing. I have since learned that when a strong Brand Strategy is created *first* and then executed clearly and consistently—even in the most subtle ways—it can pack a huge punch.

Why do certain businesses and organizations delight us so much? And if we must be inundated with all these marketing messages in today's world, why can't we expect—nay, demand—more *delight*?

Effective advertising and messaging stem from strong branding. Without a strong Brand Strategy, organizations flounder, trying out different marketing tactics in order to find one that sticks.

In a way, good branding is an art form and, like any art, it has the power to inspire, delight, anger, provoke, motivate, and entertain. Good branding can transform a frumpy housewife into a triathlete (Nike), an average guy into a chick magnet (Axe), a plain Jane into graceful royalty (Tiffany & Co.), a take-out food junkie into a dinner party diva (Williams-Sonoma), or a simple accountant into a rebellious road warrior (Harley-Davidson). It can even inspire us to get involved in our communities and take an active interest in government (Barack Obama).

This ability to inspire and delight has finally been discovered in the nonprofit arena with great success. Nonprofits like The American Society for the Prevention of Cruelty to Animals (ASPCA) are realizing that the secret sauce that makes a for-profit's balance sheet look so good can apply to their own image, message, and brand. I've been lucky enough to work with nonprofits through volunteer organizations such as the Taproot Foundation (Taprootfoundation.org) and affectionately term this "using brand for good rather than evil."

A strong brand that connects with the subconscious and emotional reasons why donors give to charity can get money pouring through the doors. The APSCA's message and brand spurs millions to open their wallets to be a voice for abused and homeless animals. And guess what? For many nonprofits, the compelling benefit isn't necessarily making the world a better place; sometimes it's tapping into a donor's personal desire to simply feel good.

I've always had a personal mission to create brands that change the world. I seek to do this with every client, even if they only reach one hundred people a day. I believe organizations of all sizes can create brands that delight, inspire, and make the world a better place—in big or small ways—while still making stockholders or owners happy.

I believe simple, well-crafted, well-targeted brand messages can accomplish more with less. We've seen hundreds of examples of large companies like Apple, Virgin, and Starbucks that built their strong brands early and now attract new fans, expand into new business lines, and increase sales—seemingly without effort. And yet so many other companies chase the next best thing to get their messages heard above the din.

Small business owners often wish they could emulate the big guys, even if those guys aren't doing things well. They carry the added burden of trying to do everything themselves, from scratch, and often forsake branding in their quest to get immediate sales and keep the doors open another month. Who can blame them when one person has to be chief executive officer, accountant, operations manager, marketing manager, and in many cases, the actual producer of the goods and services they sell? When you're knee-deep in inventory control, invoicing, lease agreements, or supplier relations, branding can seem like an afterthought, or a luxury you can't afford.

My goal with this book is to help small businesses, start-ups, and even nonprofit organizations build meaningful brands that *connect* with their audiences: brands that say something about their customers and partners, extend easily into other products or services, and turn customers and partners into evangelists. They can learn these lessons by emulating large, successful companies as well as businesses right around the corner.

I'd love to see more marketing out there that doesn't insult our intelligence, waste our time, or offend our senses. I want to show you how everyone in the organization influences brand and how a complete Brand Strategy now will help you make a thousand little decisions later on, so you can reap big rewards, get that cash register to ring, appeal to new donors, and attract rabid, loyal fans.

Enjoy the ride. It'll be fun.

Part 1:
What Is Brand and Why Does It Matter?

What Is a Brand?

IN THE MID-1990s, NIKE introduced a branding and advertising campaign called *If You Let Me Play*. The ad campaign was an offshoot of their iconic *Just Do It* message. The ads showed poignant close-ups of young girls of every race saying,

"If you let me play sports
I will like myself more;
I will have more self-confidence,
If you let me play sports.
If you let me play,
I will be 60 percent less likely to get breast cancer;
I will suffer less depression.
If you let me play sports,
I will be more likely to leave a man who beats me.
If you let me play,
I will be less likely to get pregnant before I want to.
I will learn what it means to be strong.
If you let me play sports.
If you let me play sports." [1]

From a purely business perspective, Nike designed this ad to sell apparel and accessories to women. Their campaign struck a powerful chord and hit me on a visceral level, making me see Nike in a whole new light.

I admired how the message went beyond "buy our stuff." This campaign was about empowering our girls, strengthening them, saving them from abuse and self-doubt, and putting them on a healthy path to adulthood. The ad was about equality, opportunity, and challenging yourself. As I looked into the eyes of the young girls on TV, I fell in love with Nike. I wanted to support Nike and all its efforts. Despite the controversies Nike has faced over the years, I smile when I recall that campaign. I hope it saved at least one girl by giving her courage and hope.

Nike showed me that a business can have a mission-driven brand and still make money. But what is this mysterious thing called *brand* and why should we care?

Brand is your story, your core purpose, and your customer promise. Brand is your reputation—which ultimately lives in the minds of your customers. Brand is what your customers say it is, not what you say it is, but you can shape and influence it through intentional actions. A clear, consistent brand will shape your business, guide your investments, and help you grow and prosper. And regardless of budget crunches or time constraints, your small business, nonprofit, or start-up can build a strong brand just like Nike. You have a powerful story to tell and a mission to accomplish. With your advantage of being small and much closer to the customer than global corporations, you have the power to engage and inspire your audience, however large it is, and make your community or world a better place.

Think about the big guys like Nike, Disney, Virgin, and Apple. How does reading the names of these companies make you feel? What images immediately come to mind? What emotions do they evoke?

Recall a memorable shopping experience you've had. How did you respond to the store, the clerk's competence, and his behavior toward you? Was the store layout appealing or did you feel anxious, claustrophobic, and manic? How did you feel about yourself when you left the store carrying their bag? Did you feel happier, smarter, more sophisticated, or more eco-savvy—or were you embarrassed to carry around the store's logo?

That, ladies and gentlemen, is brand in action.

But what does *brand* truly mean?

Some people believe brand is merely a logo, a website, or company colors. I work with many business owners who say, "Oh, I don't need a Brand Strategy. I already have my logo and business cards, thank you." But those items are only outer symbols of the brand—vehicles that communicate your brand to the world. They are not the brand itself.

For years, Scott Montgomery, executive creative director and principal for Bradley and Montgomery (bamideas.com), a brand innovation agency, has been building and communicating brands in unique ways for the likes of Microsoft, Angie's List, and JPMorgan Chase. He also lectures frequently on branding and has been featured on National Public Radio (NPR) and in *The New York Times*. Here's what Scott has to say about brand:

> 66In a world where absolutely everything in media is changing, let me try to define 'brand' in a way that won't. A brand is exactly two things: it's the promise your offering makes to people, and the clothes that promise is dressed in. The degree to which that combination generates the behavior you want from people is all that matters.99

Brand is the core experience, the story, and the essence of your business. It's your company's reputation, personality, and reason for being—all rolled into one package.

Brand contains the promise you make to customers, the value your product or services provide, and the difference between you and your competition. Brand is your reputation, your image, and the "mind share" you occupy in people's brains based on their experiences with you, whether real or imagined.

Brand can also encompass your philosophy, a cause, and the reason you do what you do. You might think of brand as the personality and soul of an organization communicated in various ways, such as through a logo. Here is Wikipedia's definition of brand:

> 66 A brand is a collection of images and ideas representing an economic producer. Brand recognition and other reactions are created by the accumulation of experiences with the specific product or service, both directly relating to its use, and through the influence of advertising, design, and media commentary. A brand is a symbolic embodiment of all the information connected to a company, product, or service. A brand serves to create associations and expectations among products made by a producer. 99

In this definition, I especially like the phrase: *both directly relating to its use, and through the influence of advertising, design, and media commentary.* This shows us that the brand experience you create is a two-way interaction across multiple vehicles. Your brand goes beyond the advertising you push out to customers. It's also based on people's first-hand interactions with your organization.

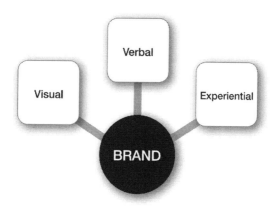

Brand communication is a three-legged stool: it is expressed not only ***visually*** (in your logo, design, or colors), but ***verbally*** (in the words you use or copy you write), and ***experientially*** as well. An ad may tell me your company is fun, convenient, and easy to do business with, but if your clerks don't smile at me or your online checkout process is akin to taking a college entrance exam, then I'm going to doubt those brand promises.

Since brand is a promise, a reputation, *and* an actual experience, entities besides businesses can have a brand. For example, countries and cities have brands. What feeling do you get when you hear Paris, France, versus Omaha, Nebraska? How about Antarctica versus Puerto Rico? I recently heard China is launching a rebranding effort to change their image on the world stage. Chinese authorities are going to highlight their scenic areas, corporate visitor centers, and museums in an effort to make the country seem more modern and welcoming.

In an October 2009 article for *CorpComms Magazine,* Alfredo Muccino, the chief creative officer of Liquid Agency, a global branding firm, explained that London's brand is no longer the quaint "royal family/tea and crumpets" deal or the "British punk movement." He feels England has morphed into something more cosmopolitan, blending the old and the new in a unique way.[2]

Events and holidays also have brands that evoke images and emotions. Take Christmas, for example. Many of us envision gathering with family and friends, decorating a tree, exchanging gifts, eating too much, and playing games with the kids. For some, Christmas has a warm, loving feeling attached to that brand. But since brand is defined by our own experiences, others may have a quite different take: to them, the brand of Christmas may represent chaos, budget woes, or stress. The brand is your own experience of that event.

People, from politicians to movie stars, may have their own brands. Famous personalities know the brand must be protected at all costs, which is why they're upset when photos are used without permission. Oprah's brand is a Midas touch for the books, people, and products she endorses. She zealously guards her media properties to protect her personal brand. No one besides Oprah appears on the cover of *O Magazine*, and her brand communicates exactly what she intends it to communicate.

We've all seen what can happen when a personal brand is tarnished by scandal, as with golfer Tiger Woods and politician John Edwards. Once a brand goes bad, it's difficult to recover from the damage.

Brand Identity Crisis

Do you ever feel frustrated when a company brags about great customer service, then traps you for thirty-five minutes on a call center help line from hell? Then you know what I mean. How about food that's branded as wholesome but turns out to be extremely high in sugar or sodium, or automobiles that claim safety as their first priority but in reality possess potentially fatal flaws?

When a brand's reality fails to live up its promise, we have a *brand identity crisis.*

When a brand's reality fails to live up its promise, we have a *brand identity crisis.* Since brand lives in the minds of customers, they are the ones who ultimately control the brand perception based on their actual experiences, no matter what you might say in your ads or tout on your website. And if you're suffering from a brand identity crisis, they will form a different impression than the one you *want* them to have about you. In these days of social media, people can now expose brand identity crises to millions of people with the click of a mouse. Even the smallest misalignment can undo what months and years of brand marketing have promised.

> The only way to have direct influence on your brand perception and avoid an identity crisis is to make a clear promise and then be certain everything you deliver and communicate is aligned with that promise.

The only way to have direct influence on your brand perception and avoid an identity crisis is to make a clear promise and then be certain everything you deliver and communicate is aligned with that promise. The rest depends on how customers perceive your intentions. If you've intentionally built a Brand Strategy that speaks directly to what those customers need and care about (rather than what *you* need or care about) and you're set up to deliver, then you should be okay.

Brand Myths Shattered

If you're part of a small business, nonprofit, or start-up with limited resources, you may think a killer brand is beyond your grasp. Not true! Let's dispel a few common myths right now.

Myth #1: Branding is difficult and time-consuming

Branding isn't rocket science, but it does require focused thought about what your business stands for and who you want to reach. Then, you must commit to consistently convey that message through everything you do. This actually saves time and effort, because you won't need to reinvent the wheel with each new activity or program. Sure, spending time up front on the ten Brand Strategy questions in Part 2 may take some time, but it is well worth the effort.

I advise you to get your Brand Strategy in place early, so you can put it into action. No lengthy six-month projects or heavy binders of recommendations for me. True, this process is never "done," because you never stop being a steward of your brand once everything is in place. But instead of starting from scratch with each new program, you simply keep an eye on things and regularly do a "system check" on your materials, business practices, customers, and messaging to ensure your brand is clear and consistent.

Branding should not be a complex process that requires a PhD. This is a simple strategy that helps you define and live your organization's values—and also provides a roadmap so employees and partners can verbalize and live those values, too. Living your values, if they're authentic to your organization's core mission, should not be hard. You know what they are; now you need to intentionally decide how to communicate them through everything you do and say. Effective branding means avoiding hypocrisy and being consistent with your employees, customers, and partners.

> Effective branding means avoiding hypocrisy and being consistent with your employees, customers, and partners.

A well-thought-out Brand Strategy makes things easier for you by getting everyone on the same page.

Myth #2: Branding is expensive

Effective branding can be achieved on any budget.

I've worked with twelve-million-dollar budgets and one-thousand-dollar budgets and no company ever thinks they have enough money, regardless of their size. The real key to effective branding is identifying a clear picture of your ideal customers and developing a benefit-driven message that speaks directly to their needs. Once you align customers and benefits, you can work with a designer to create your logo and visual identity and with a writer to craft your copy.

Branding only becomes expensive when you *don't* take time to build a clear Brand Strategy first, because then you're grasping at straws and throwing money away on activities that don't move you forward. An irresistible brand is not about big budgets; it's about making a promise your target audience cares about, then delivering on it clearly and consistently across all customer touchpoints.

Brand is not about big budgets; it's about making a promise your target audience cares about, then delivering on it clearly and consistently across all customer touchpoints.

That is what makes branding effective, not how much you spend. Thousands of customer touchpoints and interactions are available to help you communicate your brand promise for free or with little added investment if you get creative. And today, with so many free communication technologies at your disposal, the only cost is time. If you're guided by a strong Brand Strategy, you will ultimately spend less money by doing the right things, rather than wasting money on the wrong things.

Myth #3: Branding is all fluff

Brand equity can make or break a company. If you think brand has no financial impact, consider why private equity firms purchase brands for billions of dollars just to gain control of the brand cache or loyal customer base. Studies tell us a strong brand image leads to increased sales, greater gross margin, and improved ROI (return on investment).[3] Taking the time to build a strong brand helps organizations survive in an economic downturn. One study showed that "strong brands enabled companies to endure continued economic weakness and thrive in the transition to recover."[4]

Brand is the reason people pay three times as much for a white T-shirt at Nordstrom than they would at Target. It's the reason people ask for Coke at a restaurant, then order water if the place only serves Pepsi. And it's the reason the exact same couch may seem hip and sleek at Pottery Barn, but appear boring and plain at a discount store. An effective brand directly translates into bottom-line sales.

> An effective brand directly translates into bottom-line sales.

If you build a brand and communicate it to the right people at the right time, you'll attract the interested customers you seek. In addition, a strong brand guides other marketing decisions that fuel your company's growth, including where to advertise, who to partner with, and how to price your product. Those decisions are anything but fluff; they are the lifeblood of your organization.

Myth #4: All designers are the same

All designers are not the same. While you can save a lot of money by thinking through a Brand Strategy on your own, you'll need a good designer to bring the visual aspects to life and make your brand appealing. Some designers get it, while others don't. When I worked for a corporation and hired outside vendors, I always turned to the right designer for advice instead of relying on someone's nephew, a high school art student, or an in-house computer programmer.

If a prospective designer doesn't ask about your target audience and what you'd like to convey to your customers and clients, then you should run the other way. A designer who only charges $100 can cost you a lot more money in lost sales by not communicating the right message. Likewise, don't ask one of your software developers to create a logo or website simply because he knows Adobe Illustrator or HTML programming. Just as someone who knows how to put pen to paper may not be a good writer, programmers are not graphic designers or branding consultants.

Graphic design is a skill. Good designers understand how imagery, font, color, shape, and spacing impact the subconscious connections people make about your company.

> Good designers understand how imagery, font, color, shape, and spacing impact the subconscious connections people make about your company.

They know how to take a verbal message and communicate it visually. And they should be experienced enough to give you clear recommendations and push back if you are going in the wrong direction.

You'll be pleased with the results if you craft a strong Brand Strategy on your own first, before embarking on any design project, and then spend a bit more money to work with a gifted designer who'll get it right from the start.

Myth #5: Branding works immediately

Branding and direct response marketing are two different things. Before a brand sticks, people need to experience it over time and in different ways. After all, brand is visual, verbal, *and* experiential, as we discussed. Nike's swoosh didn't have meaning within the first three months it appeared. No one knew what Ben and Jerry were about until news of their socially responsible brand and practices started to spread. And before Disney was *Disney*, with all the imagination, magic, and family entertainment it represents, the company was just an animator named Walt Disney who had big dreams.

Starbucks began as a little-known coffee company in 1971, but in 1982 Howard Schulz began transforming the brand into the retail powerhouse we know today. Schulz made brand changes and then held fast to his vision of what Starbucks could mean to customers, community, and society in general. He never wavered as he carefully built the company's marketing and brand around that vision.

Branding and messaging evolve over time as customers respond to them. You may be tired of your brand and messaging after three months, but that doesn't mean all your potential customers have had a chance to see it and form an opinion. A marketing research guideline suggests people need to see a marketing message five to seven times before they act on it. While you may live, eat, and breathe your brand on a daily basis, others need a chance to see it more than once and respond.

> While you may live, eat, and breathe your brand on a daily basis, others need a chance to see it more than once and respond.

If the message is different every time they see it, then you're always starting from zero with your target audience. Give the brand messages and visuals time to work their magic before deciding to pull the plug. As long as your direction is focused and you're consistent across media, you should give the brand concept six months to one year to heat up before you decide if it's working or not.

Avoid the temptation to change things every few months in an effort to boost quarterly sales growth. If you spend time up front making the best decisions about your Brand Strategy *before* you implement it, then you won't feel the need for major changes later.

Think long and hard before you flip the switch on a logo or brand positioning.

If you get consistent feedback that things aren't working, then you know it's time to make a change. When Pepsi altered their Tropicana juice carton packages in 2009, the new cartons were bland and generic looking. Responding to intense public outcry, Pepsi's CMO at the time, David Burwick, conceded: "Sometimes you land in a great place, and sometimes you don't. And when you don't, you need to find a better place. Fast."[5]

Branding vs. PR vs. Marketing vs. Social Media . . . Oh My!

Along with believing brand is the same thing as a logo, people often confuse branding with public relations and marketing tactics, such as press releases, advertising, social media—even price promotions. In reality, brand forms the *foundation* of your marketing plan: it shouldn't come after the fact. Only by clarifying your Brand Strategy are you able to make the right decisions, such as if and where to advertise, whether to buy a booth at a particular event, and where to send press releases.

With that in mind, let's put definitions around these terms to keep things straight. Think of this as Marketing 101.

Branding and Marketing Are Not the Same

If any of you suffered through business school as I did, you learned about the ***Four P's of Marketing—product, price, place, and promotion:***

1. **Product (or Service):** What do we sell and how do we make it?
2. **Price:** How much do we charge for it?
3. **Place:** Where and how do we get it to our end consumers?
4. **Promotion:** How do we get people to know it exists and convince them to buy it?

So, broadly, marketing is an umbrella term for bringing products or services to "market" and effectively selling them. Too often, small business owners only think of marketing in terms of the fourth P, Promotion. But marketing encompasses so much more. Subcategories that fall under marketing include:

- Advertising
- Communications
- Database marketing
- Direct marketing
- Event organization
- Field marketing
- Global marketing
- International marketing
- Online marketing
- Mobile marketing
- Industrial marketing
- Market research
- Public relations
- Product marketing
- Media /Press relations
- Retailing
- Lead generation
- Search engine marketing
- Social influence marketing
- Social media
- Pricing
- Market research
- Competitive analysis

Organizations roll all the associated strategies and tactics within these subcategories into a collective *marketing plan*. The marketing plan covers the tactics and themes each group will execute during the year: Which ads will be placed, where will those ads go, and what will be the main messages? On which markets will we focus? What products will we promote at different times of the year? What is the product release schedule? What is the competition doing this year? What customer-acquisition campaigns will take place? Which events will we sponsor?

> Brand forms the foundation of your overall marketing strategy but is not the *same thing* as a marketing strategy. Brand touches much more than marketing and can serve as a litmus test for your operations, hiring practices, distribution strategy, and partner selection.

Brand forms the foundation of your overall marketing strategy but is not the *same thing* as a marketing strategy. Brand touches much more than marketing and can serve as a litmus test for your operations, hiring practices, distribution strategy, and partner selection.

People often believe advertising and branding are interchangeable and mean the same thing. They don't. Advertising is a marketing tactic based on the Brand Strategy. Advertising is but one vehicle to communicate your brand message to the world. Brand positioning should be thought out *before* you create an advertisement.

The beauty of owning a small business is that things are far less complicated and you have a huge opportunity to get this right where the big guys might trip up. If you're new and just launching a business, this is the perfect time to build your Brand Strategy. Determine the brand *before* you create a marketing plan, so you won't spend precious time and money chasing your tail.

As a small business owner, you don't need a complicated marketing plan. A Brand Strategy can show you what you do and don't need. Being small means you're close to your customers and all decisions are made by you. This means you call the shots and can ensure all the pieces align. Being nimble and small are strengths and can help you build your brand the right way from the start.

Branding Is Not Public Relations

To keep it simple, think of public relations (PR) as media, awards, and speaking engagements. Public relations means communicating information to various audiences, downplaying negative information, and elevating positive information in order to improve your company's reputation and credibility. As one implement in your "promotion toolbox," PR activities are *a part of* your marketing plan, not the same thing as the marketing plan.

But PR targets different audiences and has different metrics and intended outcomes than other marketing tactics you may use. Since PR is about getting third parties to talk about you, it tends to be viewed as more credible than paid advertising. For example, a targeted PR campaign might establish your company or executives as trusted experts in the field. Radio interviews, local TV appearances, public speaking engagements, award submissions, and contributed online and offline articles for media publications fit this category.

The goal of PR is to establish credibility and get your organization's name out there—perhaps by educating your target audience about your products and services in a softer way than pure advertising. But keep in mind that PR won't necessarily create new customers for your products because it isn't a direct marketing channel. While PR certainly helps make your direct marketing efforts more effective, if you expect an immediate correlation with increased sales, you may be disappointed.

Many small business owners think PR activity is synonymous with "marketing plan" or even branding. I've heard too many small business owners say: "My marketing or Brand Strategy this year is to do four press releases each month." A marketing plan should include much more than simply a steady stream of press releases. As I hope I've shown, PR is only one tactic within your larger marketing plan.

The Brand Strategy shapes your PR messages and target-media lists. If brand is the story you tell, then PR is about amplifying that story. It increases your exposure by linking your organization to timely news stories or trends. What PR cannot do is create a brand where none exists, or worse, make people think your brand is something it's not. That might work for a little while, but your customers will soon catch on.

Back in 2008, Karen Hughes, former communications advisor to George W. Bush, took a job at high-profile PR firm Burston Marstellar.[6]

The article stated that Hughes "left her State Department position ... after making little progress on her mission to improve the U.S. image around the world." Seems the government expected her to battle global image problems by applying a coating of good press—and it was surprised when that didn't quite come to pass. This was in 2008, when the United States' "brand" was taking a global beating. Wow. Talk about an uphill battle. No wonder PR gets a bad rap—people expect it to perform miracles.

Here's the thing: PR can't just come along and make you thinner, prettier, or more popular if the fundamentals aren't in place—if the *brand promise* isn't met. Many CEOs think they can operate poorly, slap a coat of public relations over everything, and their reputation will be magically transformed. Brand doesn't work that way. Public relations can bring good things to light and even downplay bad things, but it won't conjure up news or goodwill from thin air. You'd be better off hiring a magician.

Back to Karen Hughes. *The Wall Street Journal* article went on to say, "despite traveling around the globe—sometimes accompanied by U.S. sports stars—and beefing up the public-diplomacy budget, Ms. Hughes wasn't able to change the world's view of the U.S., according to polls."

I'm not making any political statements here, but all companies can learn a lesson from this. People aren't as stupid as we'd like to believe, and it's best not to try and force-feed a message to them. You can say something over and over, but if you haven't delivered on that clear brand promise—if poor product choices, bad environmental practices, or rude customer service have been the status quo—then no amount of well-placed media articles and glossy movie-star parades will change that.

In the end, it all comes down to your organization's DNA and what your customers—and employees—see and experience. Are you consistently *living* your brand promise?

> Are you consistently *living* your brand promise?

Companies that think good PR will erase broken promises are kidding themselves. If it were that easy, everyone would be doing it. If your brand experience isn't clear and consistent, no amount of PR can make people think it is, just because you say so.

Branding Is Not Social Media

(ring, ring)

Me: "Red Slice, Maria speaking."

Client: "Hi, Maria. My name is Sue and I own a small business here in town. I've heard you're one of the best branding experts on the planet *[Note: artistic license taken during this reenactment]*. I'm looking for branding help."

Me: "Excellent! Why don't you tell me a bit about your goals and what you want to achieve?"

Client: "Well, I hear social media is all the rage and I need to get in on that. Can I hire you to build my Facebook fan page?"

Me: "We have great Facebook partners if that's what you need, but it's best to work on your Brand Strategy first and talk about your benefits, differentiators, and your target audience. Then we can decide if Facebook is actually the right platform for you. Having the Brand Strategy helps you spend your limited marketing dollars and time wisely."

Client: "But, that's what I'm saying. I know my Brand Strategy. It's to build a Facebook fan page."

Me: "Okay, so tell me a bit about what your brand is all about. What's your mission and who is your ideal customer?"

Client: "I sell those modified mobile phones. You know, the ones with the big numbers and really simple functions for elderly people who can't see very well. Many of those folks are tech-averse and don't need all the bells and whistles on their phone. So when can we start on a Facebook fan page? Oh, and can you help with Twitter, too?"

Me: "Well, Facebook and Twitter are just tactics—part of an overall marketing plan. And the marketing plan is based on a strong Brand Strategy. Putting all of that aside, may I ask if the folks buying these phones are on Facebook and Twitter? With their sight issues and dislike of technology, are they even on social media?"

Client: "Well, isn't everyone on Facebook and Twitter these days?"

Me: "Many people are, but if you're working with a limited budget, I'm not sure Facebook and Twitter are the best ways to reach the specific people who need your product. It would help to sit down and walk through your Brand Strategy, which includes looking at your ideal buying audience. Then, we can hone in on the best choices for your time and money."

Client: "Well, I'm not sure I have the time or money for all that. I just want to get the Facebook fan page and Twitter thing going, because I keep hearing that's how to get customers."

You can see where this is going.

Social media is not hype or a fad. It has forever changed brand relationships by creating two-way conversations between company and customer that leads to more loyalty and, ultimately, more purchases.

Starbucks has great success with social media and uses it to launch new products and promotions via its rabid online evangelists. Many of their ideal customers are tech-savvy and heavy social-media users. I once heard Starbucks' "official Twitterer" speak at a luncheon. He said social media is an effective way for them to monitor new product feedback, make corporate changes, conduct launches, and even adapt customer service. Beats the old Suggestion Box any day of the week.

Companies that are open and agile can leverage social media and react in a heartbeat to suggestions and crises.

But I stand behind this mantra: Social media is not a Brand Strategy. It is *part of* your Brand Strategy.

> Social media is not a Brand Strategy. It is *part* of your Brand Strategy.

Social media is just one avenue (albeit a unique, interactive, viral one) through which you communicate your brand to the world. As I like to tell clients and audiences: "Starting a Twitter account is not a marketing plan or Brand Strategy. It is merely part of one."

Social media may not be right for every company. I know dozens of great social-media strategists who give sound advice, do great work, and know how to leverage Twitter, Facebook, and the rest. I often recommend my clients work with them—but only if the client's Brand Strategy points to social media as an effective vehicle.

Even social media experts agree that you should have a fully-baked Brand Strategy *before* you dive into execution. You have to know what story you're telling and to whom before putting it out there.

I might be a lone voice in the wind on this one, but I don't believe *every* company needs a Twitter account, a Facebook fan page, or even a blog. **It all depends on your target audience and your brand promise.** You need to communicate your brand through vehicles that will reach your target audience and be effective. If they use social media to interact with brands like yours, then absolutely, you should extend your brand to those channels. We'll talk more about choosing the right channels in Part 3 of the book.

In addition, if your Brand Strategy isn't well thought-out, then how do you know what to communicate in these social media vehicles? Social media should *extend* the messaging expressed through your other marketing activities; it doesn't live in isolation. Brand is the content. Social media is the context or channel.

Here's another big issue with social media: it can be unforgiving if you create an inauthentic relationship—a loosey-goosey brand promise with no substance behind it. Scott Montgomery sees many companies using social media the wrong way, with transparent "seeded" comments and overly-pushy promotional messages that are all one-sided. Talk about getting kicked off the island. Not only is Scott grounded in brand fundamentals, he's also co-founder of Fizziology (Fizziology.com), a company that tracks, analyzes, and mines social media chatter. He sees the biggest branding successes in social media from **enthusiast brands:** " . . . those that can offer value through social engagement, and those that are creating a bit of controversy. Many brands win in social media not just because they engage in it, but by the fact that their innovations are worth tweeting about. I'm certainly not ruling out some kinds of seeding, but it's all the more powerful if you devise your product's strategy to be inherently 'political.' By that, I mean create things where the audience has a reason to take your side (or at least *a* side). Let your product efforts, promotions, and events be retweetable."[7]

If this book does anything for you, I hope it convinces you that branding and marketing aren't the same thing, that promotion and PR are not the only aspects of marketing, and that social media *extends* a strong brand, but it is not a Brand Strategy in and of itself. Now that we're all speaking the same language, we'll explore why Brand Strategy matters to your business.

Why Does Brand Matter?

What can brand do for you? Just as we respect and admire people who know who they are and what they want, brand helps organizations attract the right customers and make sales more easily. Brand *clarity* attracts customers and brand *consistency* makes them stick around.

> Brand *clarity* attracts customers and brand *consistency* makes them stick around.

As customers encounter your brand in various situations they'll remember you, slot you into the right part of their brains, and your brand will stick. The more you fulfill the brand promise in everything you do, the more you'll solidify your brand to the people who matter most. Your Brand Strategy is the tool that helps you accomplish this. For every business decision, you should ask yourself, "Does this accurately reflect my brand to the customers I want to attract?" If the answer is no, then don't do it!

In addition, a strong Brand Strategy enables you to do more with less. Rather than wasting money and time on the wrong activities, a Brand Strategy helps you laser-focus on activities and messages that will have the greatest impact.

> Rather than wasting money and time on the wrong activities, a Brand Strategy helps you laser-focus on activities and messages that will have the greatest impact.

With the tight budgets and time constraints common to small businesses, startups, and nonprofits, this is a necessity. Brand Strategy isn't about quantity—it's about quality. Even if you can only afford limited marketing activities, a strong Brand Strategy will help you make sure each of them packs a powerful punch.

What's Your Reason for Being?

When it comes right down to it, we're in business to make money. But unless you know the true essence of what your business is all about and its impact on people's lives, you'll be stuck on the lowest rung of the ladder. In a competitive market where many new businesses fail, that's a death sentence.

Marty Neumeier, director of transformation at Liquid Agency (Liquidagency.com) and author of *The Brand Gap* and *Zag* suggests giving yourself the Obituary Test to figure out your reason for being: write the obituary of your organization in twenty-five years and outline what it did that was great and why the world is a better place because it existed.

"When you do this, you see something bigger. You see how every symbol, message, and action you put out into the world creates a brand legacy in the minds of customers, which is really where brand lives in the first place," Marty says. He advises this will not only attract the right employees to grow your business, but will impact everything you do. "When you open a business just to make money, you can lose heart."

Please don't overcomplicate how you express your reason for being. It doesn't have to be big, momentous, or heavy. Alexandra Franzen, a communication specialist and author of *50 Ways to Say You're Awesome* (Sourcebooks), advises that the clearest way to express an idea is best. "Think about the last time you read a blog post, heard a TED Talk or listened to a story at a dinner party that really impacted you, that made you want to do something," she asks. "Was it long, convoluted, unnecessarily detailed? Or was it simple, clear, direct and conversational?" Alexandra adds, "Writing about the work that you do—your 'reason for being'—is a form of storytelling. And if you want to inspire people to take action, a simple story is best."

In her work with entrepreneurs, she finds that many people—especially those with a purpose-driven, passion-driven business—

get overwhelmed when it comes to describing their work. Many business owners feel their "reason for being" ought to be "bigger" or "more complex" than it actually is, she says. But again: simplicity is best.

"Maybe you're an illustrator and your 'reason for being' is to add more beauty to the world. How refreshingly simple is that?" suggests Alexandra. "Or maybe you're a yoga teacher and your 'reason for being' is that you'd like to help one thousand people in your lifetime feel more comfortable in their own skin. Once you release the idea that your 'reason for being' has to be dense or complicated, it's like a huge weight off your shoulders. Things start to make sense—for you, and your audience, too."

When writing about our businesses, we tend to overcomplicate and seek something that sounds big and meaningful, when what is really meaningful is often expressed in the simplest way.

A clear Brand Strategy, based on your larger reason for being, makes it easier to focus your organization's activities around one true cause. It helps you easily determine which products or services to offer, how to price them, what your logo should convey, what experience your website should evoke, and even which people to hire. Making such decisions without a strong brand foundation is akin to throwing darts at a moving target. You'll waste time and money with designers, website programmers, and writers because either everything will look good, or nothing will. Without a guidepost, any road looks like the right one, even if it leads to a dead end!

Building a Brand That Can Change with the Times

A tried-and-true business strategy is to ask yourself what business you are actually in. An old adage asks: "Are you in the horse-and-buggy business or the transportation business?" In the early

1900s, many companies in *the horse-and buggy-business* went under when automobiles came out. But if you were in the *transportation business,* you could have changed course and started offering automobiles or branched into something else transportation-related. If you clung to the horse-and-buggy business, then you didn't understand your customers' true needs. People didn't need buggies per se—they needed a way to grandma's house on Christmas Eve. The lesson: don't put yourself in a box, leaving no room to adapt and grow.

This kind of thinking allows you to understand and meet your customers' needs. As Red Slice, I help organizations and people tell their stories. My mission is to engage, inform, and delight audiences. This approach inspires my clients and helps me do a better job for them. It also separates me from my competition, which just offers marketing services.

If your brand can address a fundamental need, then you can see things through your customer's eyes and this kind of positioning will inspire customer loyalty beyond your imagination.

Ever see the movie *Jerry Maguire?* In one scene, Dorothy (Renee Zellweger) agrees to leave the security of a bigger agency and follow Jerry (Tom Cruise) to his new, independent sports agency venture—all because of Jerry's mission statement. The new mission statement defined the true role of sports agents: to stop being driven by money and spend more time helping clients achieve their dreams. When Dorothy explains why she took a chance and went to work with him, she says, "Mostly, I just want to be inspired."

Inspiration is something we all crave. Human beings want to know, consciously or subconsciously, that their efforts are going toward a higher purpose. Even a small dose of inspiration can ignite a sense of purpose and get people to do amazing things for the good of the company and its customers.

A Brand Strategy can lead to this inspiration, because it gives your business a mission and a vision. I've worked for startup firms that considered Brand Strategy a "fluffy" component and only cared about taking the company public. Not only did these workplaces lack soul and heart, they also had no rudder to help us determine the most effective marketing strategies. So we focused on a feature war with competitors ("We have this new widget." "Oh, yeah? Well, we have that widget, *plus two more!*")

As employees, we had no idea why we were putting in thankless twelve-hour days. If you can't delight and inspire your employees, you won't be able to delight and inspire customers.

These example questions will help you focus on the "higher calling" of your business:

- Are you a graphic designer, OR do you solve your clients' communication challenges?
- Do you sell baby clothes, OR do you help mothers pass on a sense of style to their children?
- Do you make computers and technology, OR do you challenge the status quo (hello, Apple)?
- Are you a jewelry designer, OR do you create memories?

Don't become so esoteric that no one can tell what you actually do, but you do need to separate yourself from the pack and go in at a deeper level to withstand market changes and commoditization. In other words, go beyond generic marketing messages such as "increase profits" or "reduce costs."

Check out this boilerplate from one of Apple's recent press releases:[8]

> "Apple designs Macs, the best personal computers in the world, along with OS X, iLife, iWork and professional software. Apple leads the digital music revolution with its iPods and iTunes online store. Apple has reinvented the mobile phone with its revolutionary iPhone and App Store, and is defining the future of mobile media and computing devices with iPad."

According to this, Apple leads revolutions, reinvents, and defines the future. Definitely more inspiring than "manufactures computers, digital devices and mobile phones," isn't it? Do Apple's competitors occupy the same space in people's brains and are they in the same "business?"

Tom Asacker, a prominent brand speaker and author (Acleareye. com) verbalizes the idea of purpose and motivation when he writes:

> **"**People are not inspired by your pursuits or your status. They're inspired—and come to life—by their pursuits. They want their work and their lives to be stimulating, meaningful, and to make a difference to others. Nietzsch wrote, 'He who has a why to live can bear with almost any how.' Without a why—a why to reach and stretch, a why to proffer ideas, a why to treat customers and coworkers with love and respect, a why to go the extra mile, a why to be committed to excellence, a why to go to work in the morning— all the hows, whats, whens, and what fors become empty rhetoric.**"**

Rabid Fans: Your Logo Should Be My Tattoo

Companies that completely understand their brand are the ones who connect with customers and inspire loyalty.

I once heard a great story from consultant and speaker Simon Sinek (startwithwhy.com) at an entrepreneur's conference. Midway through his presentation, he polled the audience of women business owners:

"How many of you have your company logo tattooed on your body?"

Amused, we looked around to see if anyone raised a hand.

"Seriously, how many of you have your company logo tattooed on your body?"

Nervous laughter rose from the crowd. A bead of sweat broke out on my forehead. Should I be saying yes? But that was preposterous!

As Simon continued, he asked us to think about bikers who sport a Harley-Davidson tattoo. Oh, now it made sense! Yes, I've seen the tattoo on many a passing motorcyclist in the Northern California hills. And then I connected the dots. That Harley tattoo is just another company logo. Customers feel such fierce loyalty to the brand that they ink themselves with the company's logo permanently. The brand means something to them and says something about their identity. They're part of the Harley "tribe." Talk about rabid fans. Those tattoo-inked customers are the best salespeople the company could ask for—and Harley doesn't pay them a dime. What business wouldn't want customers who pay out of their own pockets to become walking billboards, and not only that, loyally purchase more and more products? You think the guy or gal with a permanent Harley tattoo will be swayed by Honda's or Suzuki's advertising? Heck no.

When was the last time you felt so strongly about a product that you tattooed the logo on your arm? The very thought of people running around with Taco Bell or Walmart tattoos makes me giggle. But Harley riders feel a connection, a kinship, with the brand that only vaguely has to do with motorcycles. It means so much more. Harley is about freedom, rebellion, the open road, adventure, strength, and camaraderie.

> That's the power of a strong brand promise. The promise is more than a product; it's a statement, a reputation, and lifestyle that resonates with customers.

That's the power of a strong brand promise. The promise is more than a product; it's a statement, a reputation, and lifestyle that resonates with customers. When you create a "tribe" for your product or service, word-of-mouth marketing becomes a snap, because tribe members influence one another.

Don't Leave It to Chance: People Will Form Their Own Brand Impressions

Every company has a brand, whether they know it or not. As stated earlier, brand is the "mind share" you take up in someone's brain—the part that lights up when they hear your name, see your logo, or buy your product. And guess what? Even if you believe this is a bunch of marketing mumbo jumbo, let me be clear: People will form an opinion about your business no matter what you do or don't do. No matter what action you take, they'll assign you a brand and form an opinion. Doesn't it make prudent business sense to get in front of that and influence the brand, so you can be sure it fits your business goals?

I once worked for a dot com during the Internet boom of the late 1990s. We were a competitor to E-Loan and Lending Tree and offered online loans and credit cards. This dot com didn't survive the bust for several reasons, but that's for another book. One thing we did well was build a strong brand. This was exciting to do from scratch, the right way, from day one—before we crafted any ads, logos, or messaging.

Back in those early Internet days, people didn't trust their financial data to online sites, so we needed to build a brand of trust and warmth to get people to share their precious information. After a strong Brand Strategy and research effort—before any advertising was conceived or produced—we created four distinct audience profiles and strategic positioning to represent where we fit against our competition. Visually, we chose yellow as our primary color to stand out from other traditional institutions that tended to use green or blue. Research told us yellow was the color most closely associated with customer advocacy. We used illustrations on the site rather than photos, and we adopted a casual tone in our copy to lend a safe, warm, whimsical air.

We competed not only with other online lending sites, but also with the traditional image of big, bad banks—overweight, balding, white-male fat cats behind mahogany desks. These hallowed institutions screamed stiff, formal, and foreboding and only let people into "the club" who looked and sounded just like them. We wanted to be the welcoming brand of "Yes" where even disenfranchised customers rejected by traditional banks would be treated fairly and find a loan or credit card just for them. We wanted good, honest, hardworking people who were intimidated by "the club" to find a place that cared about them and would help them achieve their dreams.

The marketing team endured heated arguments with certain engineers and programmers who thought the resulting brand was fluffy, cartoonish, and unnecessary. They fought us at every turn as we tried to inject this brand into the website design, the advertising strategy, and the PR outreach. Internally, we even trained our call center staff on the brand to ensure they adopted the right tone on the telephone with customers. I'll never forget the words of one senior technical executive who sniffed, "Look at Google. Look at Craig's List. They're simple black and white interfaces that get results. We look like clowns. People just want credible information and to get data, period. They don't need bells and whistles."

But he failed to see that being "functional" and "utilitarian" is still a brand choice. Google and Craig's List worked well in simple formats because it fit their brand promise at the time. Google's clean interface of a search box and a small graphic communicated "No muss, no fuss" in finding exactly what you were looking for within the vast Internet labyrinth. That was their brand promise and the interface delivered it. Craig's List was trying to move people from newspaper classifieds to the web in a big way. They needed basic categories like a newspaper, since all posts were user-generated ads. They wanted to be the "no-frills, grassroots, power-to-the-people, community-based-technology-for-the-rest-of-us" brand.

Google and Craig's List didn't ask people to invest a high level of personal, confidential data. We, on the other hand, tried to convince customers who didn't trust traditional banks in the first place to not only perform financial functions online, but to feel comfortable sharing sensitive financial data with us. And in 1999, this was something most people just didn't do. So, we needed to create a brand that was (a) different from the industry that had rejected them in the past and (b) approachable, warm, and inviting.

I can proudly say that this strategy would have been extremely effective—had the company not gone under due to other causes. Based on this strong Brand Strategy, the advertising increased our loan application rates by over 100 percent in our 14 target markets, just two weeks into the multi-channel ad campaign based on radio spots alone; the TV, print, and billboard components hadn't even hit those markets yet. I've chuckled over the years as traditional banks have adopted an almost identical Brand Strategy, some even using our "yes" verbiage.

Here's another example. My husband and I want to love and support a special local bookstore in our neighborhood. Based on location, name, and visual identity, the store promises a warm, personal, book-buying experience unlike the big box bookstores. Unfortunately, my husband was turned off by an incident that didn't seem important at the time. One day when we entered the store, someone behind us left the door open as we walked in and they walked out. The clerk glanced up, saw the open door, and headed over in a huff to close it. Her body language told us she was miffed and assumed we were to blame. She nearly pushed us out of the way in her haste to make a point and shut the door. How was that attitude personal and warm?

I'm sure the storeowner didn't *mean* for this to be our experience, but that owner failed to ensure his employees were warm and friendly. Because one clerk didn't live up to the store's brand, we now have a negative perception of the place as snooty and cold. At first my husband couldn't figure out why shopping there made him uncomfortable, but then he recalled this seemingly insignificant incident.

The lesson to small business owners is this: Since brand is experience, perception, and "mind share," you're going to have a brand whether you mean to or not. And every little choice you make or don't make will affect that brand.

> Since brand is experience, perception, and "mind share," you're going to have a brand whether you mean to or not. And every little choice you make or don't make will affect that brand.

People will file your business away in certain parts of their brain, as humans tend to do when processing information. They're going to make assumptions about you and decide if you're right for them. Are you for tweens or old ladies? Do you represent high-end, lasting quality or trendy and cheap?

As customers interact with your business in hundreds of different ways, they will form opinions and tell their friends. Wouldn't you rather influence their perception with a consistent message and experience, rather than leave it up to fate? I know I would.

How to Avoid Random Acts of Marketing: Brand Strategy as Your Foundation

Without a Brand Strategy, how the heck can you decide:
- what to offer and to whom
- how to price it
- what colors or graphics to use in your logo, based on what you want to communicate
- what tone your copy needs to take

- what publications to advertise in
- what type of employees to hire
- which partners to play with?

If you don't have a grounded Brand Strategy, you're all over the place, grasping at whatever new trend or opportunity is in front of you on any given day. I call this "performing random acts of marketing." And if you're confused, don't you think customers will feel the same? Let me ask it this way: Would you put up drywall and build a façade for a house with no foundation poured or studs in place? You have to do one thing before the other or the whole structure will collapse. Same principle with brand.

Marketing Programs and Tactics
Create needed materials.
Decide where to advertise, promote.

Brand Building Blocks

Visual Identity

Company Name

Key Messages

Brand Strategy

Who are we?   Who is my ideal customer?
Where are they?   How are we different?
What is our personality?   What is our promise?

The previous figure illustrates a good way to look at Brand Strategy and what it can do for you. You'll see that building the Brand Strategy first creates a firm foundation. We'll explore that foundation through the key Brand Strategy questions in Part 2 of this book.

The Brand Strategy questions are designed to help you think about who you serve, what you represent, why you're different, and what value you offer. They also help you focus on your ideal customer. If you don't know who and where your buyers are, you'll spend time and money on the wrong things and end up poking your eye out with a sharp stick in frustration because nothing will work.

Brand as Investment Guidepost

You have a great business idea. So you immediately contact a marketing consultant or designer and request the following:

- Logo
- Website
- Brochures
- Business cards
- Letterhead

Hold on a sec. Yes, those are basic marketing communication pieces, but without factoring in your ideal audience and the way they need to interact with your brand, how do you know if you need all these elements? For example, I communicate with all my clients over email. Do I need to print thousands of sheets of linen letterhead that will only be scanned, emailed, and never appreciated? Will customers find you through referrals from friends who've already seen and experienced your product? If that's the case, do you need a 15-page brochure when a one-page PDF fact sheet will fill in the blanks for them?

Know how your customers need to find and interact with you before you create everything under the sun and end up a year from now dumping all those lovely brochures into the recycle bin.

When attending trade shows, business people assume they need printed materials on hand at the booth. Upon signing up for an event, their gut reaction is to say "What brochures will we need?" Whoa, fella. Let's take a step back. Who are the people at this show? What other sponsors will be there? How will attendees consume information? Are they flying here and already loaded down with luggage? If so, those expensive four-color brochures will end up in the hotel trashcan, and then where will you be? Are they coming specifically to see you, or will you have competition around? Maybe you only need to give people an item that will help them remember your name and drive them to more detailed information on your website.

Know thy audience and thy brand and you will know the best marketing tactics in which to invest. Translation: only pay for things that will get you more buzz among the right target audience and will ultimately lead to sales.

As the figure above shows, once you've answered the key questions and created your overall Brand Strategy, you can use the answers and data you've collected for what I call the Brand Building Blocks. These are basic items every company needs to mix and match in order to do the rest of their marketing. The building blocks include your company name if you don't already have one (and revisiting your Brand Strategy may inspire you to change it), your visual identity (logo, colors, imagery), and key messages. Based on your benefits and audience, for example, you can select a meaningful name that's memorable, easy to spell and pronounce, stands out from your competition, and communicates something about your values, benefits, and differentiating factors to your target audience. Or you can choose company colors that resonate with your target audience, communicate the proper emotions and "feel" of your brand, or help you stand out among competitors.

If you haven't thought about your target audience in detail, you may miss choosing a name that will attract them and communicate your brand promise all by itself. Of course you'll need to check if the name is already trademarked and if the right website URL is available, but this exercise will help you select a name that has impact. Once you have the right name for your business, you'll be able to select a logo and know what key messages to craft, based on the information in your Brand Strategy. We will talk more about applying brand to these items in Part 3 of this book.

CelebriDucks, a quirky little company, became extremely successful because they articulated a unique brand promise before they even started the company. They use that strategy to guide all of their decisions, as you'll see from the Brand at Work case study that follows.

Brand at Work: CelebriDucks

A differentiated brand must be clear and fire on all cylinders in order to stand out from the crowd. This is especially true if you have a quirky, unique brand that some people may not "get." CelebriDucks (CelebriDucks.com) went all-out in creating their brand before launching the company. CelebriDucks is the original creator of the first-ever celebrity rubber ducks representing the greatest icons of film, music, athletics, and history. Are you familiar with baseball player bobbleheads? They're kind of like that. CelebriDucks have been produced for the NBA, MLB, NHL, NASCAR, NCAA collegiate mascots, and numerous Fortune 500 companies. They were voted one of the top 100 gifts by *Entertainment Weekly* and their line includes everyone from Elvis Presley and Marilyn Monroe to the world's first ever 100 percent recycled "green" duck. The company has pioneered a whole new collectible with over 200 different CelebriDucks to date.

CelebriDucks' brand is meant to be cool, whimsical, and outside the box. They appeal to someone looking for a unique, fun, and well-crafted gift. Each duck is intricately sculpted and painted and arrives in a gorgeous gift box. "We knew from the start that our brand is an attitude and our corporate point of view, reflected in the products we create," says Craig Wolfe, president. "We set out to craft the most classy, unique, and innovative rubber ducks on the market."

Cool and classy...rubber ducks? Most definitely. CelebriDucks is a higher-end brand, offering something different: they know their target customers will pay well for that one-of-a-kind experience. "When people want boring and cheap, we send them to another company," says Craig. "We are more expensive than almost every rubber duck on the market and there's a reason for it. We're different!" This brand promise extends to their decisions about distribution and advertising: they avoid being distributed in discount environments and when they advertise, they only choose high-quality partners.

Being different and unique permeates everything the company does—even product-line choices. "We never wanted to be like everyone else from day one. We knew no one did licensed rubber ducks, no one else used top-flight gift boxes for ducks, no one really cared to sculpt and paint with a detail that was unknown in the industry. And half of the ducks on the market did not even float correctly. Then along came CelebriDucks, which changed the landscape."

Their brand is so unique and well-crafted that this guided the decision to bring the manufacturing of their rubber ducks back "home" to the U.S., where it was originally invented. They are the only company manufacturing quality rubber ducks in the U.S. and they are making them for everyone from Harley-Davidson to the Future Farmers of America.

Has such a unique and bold brand paid off? You bet! The company has been featured on CNN and hundreds of other media outlets. CelebriDucks is also the only one licensed to do the mascots for the top U.S. universities, celebrities, and major film studios. Companies such as Pacific Gas & Electric and Amazon now come to them to be added to the line.

They have even expanded the brand into a new division with their Cocoa Canard brand. "Canard" is French for "duck" and this new line of high-quality chocolate dessert items ties in with their Cocoa Canard food-themed rubber ducks to offer customers a one-of-a-kind gift option. It features the highest-quality drinking chocolate and other gluten-free desserts. Creating unique and fun gifts that reflect the company's passions is what this brand extension is all about.

Such success is certainly nothing to quack at.

Brand as Asset

Brand can be a powerful asset for any business, large or small. The strongest brands can even stay alive after death. What comes to mind when you hear massage chairs and ionic air purifiers? Ah, Sharper Image. Many a boring Saturday was spent meandering around those stores and testing gadgets. But alas, the chain went bankrupt.

But wait . . . don't count them out. In 2008, two of the country's largest retail liquidators, Hilco and Gordon Brothers, resurrected the brand to live on in the virtual sense. Other retailers who want to bask in the glow of Sharper Image's hard-earned brand equity can license it to make their own gadgets more appealing.

This is the power of brand. The company name created such a strong mental association that licensing the name after the company folded is worth money. I bet when the CFOs of those liquidators cash their licensing checks, no one is saying "branding is just fluffy marketing stuff," now, are they?

Here's the part I love. The fact that Sharper Image still wanted to maintain an upscale, quality-brand association as they closed. They dictated rules around the look of the "Store Closing" signs at retail locations' close-out sales: "No bright orange signs. You can't be too schlocky," they said. Now that's a real understanding of how to maintain brand promise.[9]

While ultimately the name of the game is sales figures, I tend to think of sales as the market share or "wallet share" you get from customers. And we all know that's the most important measure of success. But brand is the "mind share" you get from customers. You'll be in a much more powerful place for long-term success if you can capture the mind share that leads to the wallet share, rather than propping up short-term results with random gimmicks, discounts, or specials that don't invite ongoing loyalty. You want a brand that elevates you above a commodity.

> You want a brand that elevates you above a commodity.

Brand as Competitive Weapon

Inside my mind lives a curmudgeonly business owner (or CEO, or VP of Engineering) named Sam. Sam thinks marketing is a bunch of hooey that wastes time and money. Sam believes goods and services are bought and sold based on quality and a conscious need—period. Let's say he sells picture frames and photo album supplies. Sam doesn't market to a particular group, because he feels anyone who takes pictures at any time might have a need for these items.

"I don't need that branding baloney," he huffs. "People who want picture frames will buy my picture frames when they need them. My products are nice-looking, good quality, and I treat people fairly. I sell the best picture and album supplies out there."

One day another business owner, Heather, also decides to sell picture frames and album supplies. She might even sell the same ones Sam does, from the same manufacturers. But as an avid photographer, Heather has a greater mission with her company: she wants to help people preserve cherished memories and imbue their personal spaces with style and personality. This immediately differentiates her from Sam. She sees picture frames as an extension of home décor, so deciding on the right ones is an important decision.

Heather carefully chooses a warm, fun, and stylish logo and colors to communicate her mission, make her company memorable, and visually appeal to the specific buying audience she has in mind. After all, photo supplies and pictures are all about being aesthetically pleasing—if her logo, colors, and entire store décor do not look good, why should anyone trust that her products will look good?

She understands that people may not consciously know why they're drawn to her, but the feelings evoked by her visual elements—her logo, colors, website, signage—have a certain design sensibility customers associate with style and flair. Customers will *want* to buy their picture frames from Heather because of what that says about their own taste and style.

Heather goes beyond the visual to live out her Brand Strategy through the customers' buying experience. Her employees are all photographers or people who have a passion for collecting and displaying photos. She even develops a training program and "checkout protocol" for her staff to ensure they offer customers advice on the best frames for certain environments or how to display an impressive photo wall. Heather offers classes at her shop for people interested in scrapbooking or photo enhancement, elevating her as a credible photo expert in the mind of her target audience. Lastly, Heather does highly targeted press outreach, only pursuing three to four key publications her target audience reads. She presents herself to the press as the area's best source for photo expertise, even if the article isn't specifically about her shop but about photography or framing in general.

Heather charges more for her picture frames than Sam. She provides more value with her welcoming shop, her expert advice, and her staff's passion—and she offers a liberal return policy should anyone be dissatisfied.

Sam is perplexed. Why would someone pay twice as much for the same frame, he wonders. We're both selling the same product to someone who has the same need: a picture frame.

But what Sam failed to grasp is that most of us make unconscious buying decisions all the time. He also failed to understand the real unconscious need of his customers, or what is called a latent or dormant need. This is a need people don't realize they have until they're presented with a better option. Sam's customers probably thought there were only so many ways to frame or display pictures, until Heather presented them with better options and styles. Remember, we all thought cassette tapes were fine until CDs came along, and CDs were fine until we found out you could store MP3s on your computer or iPod and save tons of space in your house.

Heather, on the other hand, not only brought her customers' needs to light by providing stylish options, she also fulfills this need. She speaks to these needs through her messaging, visual elements, and even her company policies and marketing activities. She addresses these needs and the benefits she provides in everything she does. Therefore, she isn't wasting money on every new marketing tactic that comes her way; she knows which will convey her brand messages and reach her target audience in the best way and which will not. So she makes wiser, more targeted use of her slim marketing budget. And she gets results.

Brand doesn't necessarily enable you to charge more for your products or services—sometimes offering the best value at the lowest price is part of the strategy. But brand does tell your story in a way that speaks to customer's subconscious needs and wants—without deceiving them in any way—so that they feel a connection. Your messages resonate more deeply with them and they tend to be more loyal as a result. In addition, this connection will cause them to tell others about you and get word of mouth going.

Sam can't merely copy aspects of Heather's business and "slap a coat of brand paint" on his own business. For example, if he tries to offer scrapbooking classes without changing anything else, will that fly? Up to this point, everything he's been saying about his business has been commodity-based and utilitarian. Will customers really believe he's the best person to help them artfully preserve their precious memories? Most likely they won't buy it, because they recognize an empty promise. We've all seen companies try to mimic a competitor, usually with disastrous results. A recent example is certain car companies trying to promote environmental responsibility and fuel-efficient models. Our experiences with these brands have shown the companies are trying to take advantage of hot trends without a real corporate commitment to the environment. I'm not saying they can't evolve as a brand or change their ways, but it will take more than slick TV ads before people change their mindset. This will happen over time as our experiences with the brand slowly change and the car company begins to fulfill its promises.

If you've been like Sam and haven't seen the bottom-line and competitive gains a strong brand can provide, there is hope. Branding succeeds when it's done *right* and when it's done *authentically*—meaning, you don't just talk the talk, but you walk the walk.

> Branding succeeds when it's done *right* and when it's done *authentically*—meaning, you don't just talk the talk, but you walk the walk.

Authentic branding can differentiate you from the competition if you stay true to it across everything you do, as it did for Outspoken Media in the Brand at Work case study below.

Brand at Work: Outspoken Media

With a name like Outspoken Media (outspokenmedia.com), you definitely need to walk your talk. This Troy, New York-based digital marketing firm does that in spades. The firm was founded by three strong, sassy women who grew tired of corporate-speak from other firms that used fluff and fake promises to gain business. The brand emphasizes being up-front, honest, transparent, and blunt in doing the right things for clients and getting results.

Visually, this shows through on their straightforward website, which focuses on the importance of growing, protecting, and managing your brand online. But Outspoken Media's brand also plays out in their business decisions, including a very selective client intake process. "Many agencies like to say they work with the best. We work with the most receptive," says Rhea Drysdale, owner and chief executive officer. "Clients need to be willing to do the hard work needed to get results without cutting corners. The SEO [search engine optimization] industry needs a better reputation; we're trying to give it one. It takes a partnership with clients to make that happen and it's vital to their brand and ours that we make the right decision to move forward."

The brand turns away international businesses and big budgets if the client isn't a good fit. One potential customer, Ross Sapir of Roadway Moving, had this to say about Outspoken Media's decision to refer him to an industry specialist rather than taking on the account themselves: "Most companies will jump on anyone who is that willing to pay $50,000 for any service. But Outspoken wanted to do the right thing. That shows their integrity and I respect that about their brand."

They refuse to compromise on the truth or their beliefs, and clients can feel good about that. The company even publicly took on a world-renowned marketing guru's brand program they thought was unfairly opt-out instead of opt-in, forcing him to change the program due to the press and public outcry. And they've spoken out against other online marketing tactics they feel are not in a business' best interest.

This company surely lives up to its name.

///

We must always remember that, as humans, not all our buying decisions are rational and binary. If that were true, the lowest price or the best product would always win in the end. But we know this isn't how the world works.

Brand Keys, a New York-based brand consulting firm, conducted a 2010 Customer Loyalty Engagement Index. According to an article in *Brandweek*,[10] they polled 33,500 consumers of 518 brands in seventy-five industry categories.

Brand Keys asked consumers detailed questions about how they relate to brands, both emotionally and rationally. Their findings show a link between brand loyalty and profitability, especially given the poor economy during that time. Robert Pasikoff, founder and president of Brand Keys, said customers want more value for their money, which means they want a strong brand for a good price. "With increased standardization and decreased product differentiation," he said, "a real brand can serve up the value consumers expect."

Pasikoff is quoted as saying we are in the "decade of the brand." In the article, he states, "This particular swing, with real brands becoming more valuable to consumers, is showing up in how they view, compare and, most importantly, buy in key categories."

The takeaway here is that human drivers don't change, whether you're Starbucks or Joe's Coffee Shack. Your brand needs to clearly communicate something, connect with customers, and show value in order to compete in a crowded marketplace.

> Your brand needs to clearly communicate something, connect with customers, and show value in order to compete in a crowded marketplace.

All Markets Have a Brand Need: Proud to Be Cheap and Disposable

Now let's look at the flip side of our fictitious photography store owner Heather's situation. Sometimes people think *brand* means expensive, as in "brand name." High cost and exquisite quality are indeed brand attributes, but you could choose to sell a generic T-shirt or dinnerware that's cheap and disposable, since certain audience segments have a real need for those items. As long as you clearly convey this message in everything you do, you can become known as *the* place to buy inexpensive white T-shirts or the most stylish, cheap, disposable dinnerware. Doesn't mean there's anything wrong with that. Fast-fashion retail brands such as H&M and Forever 21 appeal to a market that wants trendy clothing and accessories that lasts one or two seasons at a really cheap price. No one would say they are competing with Versace or Prada quality! The problem arises when you *try to be* the expensive, luxurious white T-shirt guy with a beautiful website and high prices. When people get the product, however, it's the same old cheap white T-shirt that falls apart after two washings.

The opposite might happen as well: you can have expensive, high-end products or services, but your website looks like a ten-year-old designed it, or your clerks are rude and unhelpful. Then you have a **brand consistency** problem, or what we talked about earlier as a **brand identity crisis.** You're trying to be all things to all people, which means you'll be nothing to no one. Good branding is what enables Nordstrom to make a quality white T-shirt and charge three times as much as Walmart. And the brand promise Nordstrom conveys in everything they do—from their high-quality goods to impeccable customer service—makes you trust it will indeed be better quality for the price. Nordstrom clearly and consistently communicates quality and high-end attributes in everything they do, from products to store layout to customer service.

Brand is who you are authentically, for better or worse. Whether you sell picture frames or luxury cars, it means you clearly understand the need you fill, the benefits you provide, and how you differ from the competition—and you walk your talk in everything you do.

Like people, brands can be funny, conservative, quirky, soft, simple, no-frills, or elegant. Markets have all kinds of needs. That's why well-designed, high-end, hip smartphones sell so well—and so do Snuggies and ShamWow's.

Like people, brands can be funny, conservative, quirky, soft, simple, no-frills, or elegant. Markets have all kinds of needs.

Seattle's Portage Bay Café in the following Brand at Work case study consistently emphasizes "clean food" in all that they do—and they walk their talk by delivering what they say and working with suppliers who align with that brand promise.

Brand at Work: Portage Bay Café

"Eat like you give a damn." That is the tagline—and brand philosophy—of Portage Bay Café (Portagebaycafe.com), an organic restaurant with three Seattle, Washington locations. According to owner John Gunnar, his commitment to selling organic, sustainable, and local food is all about giving customers "clean food." He targets professionals and progressive types who want to feel confident the food they consume is healthy and clean. "We target people who care about what they're eating and where it comes from," says John. And they do it all with a sense of play and lightheartedness—hence, the unconventional tagline. "Our brand is about healthy, clean, progressive living but without taking things too seriously. We like to have fun with our ads, our messages, and show that you don't have to be pretentious and uptight to enjoy healthy, clean, local food."

John learned early in his business about the power of focusing his brand on a niche audience and serving them well. He realized back in 1997 when he started with a more standard café that he was trying to be all things to all people. As an organic eater himself, John had an epiphany that he wasn't being authentic with his own business and brand. So he began integrating organics into the menu and raising prices accordingly. This was a huge gamble—but it paid off: he tripled business in a year and a half. John ensured this organic message was pervasive. In order to build the reputation and brand, he placed it on the menus, table tents, everywhere. "Our brand works because I am personally passionate about it," John says. "We go after a niche, but it's one I believe in. You have to believe in your brand and what you are doing."

Obviously, the brand plays a role when sourcing food. John only partners with suppliers that provide organic and sustainable ingredients, trying to buy locally whenever possible. And his focus on professional and progressive people who are willing to spend more to "eat clean" helps him decide on marketing tactics: Portage Bay Café sponsors a lot of sports-oriented events to attract his target demographics. John has turned down radio station ads when their listeners were not a good fit. He did, however, advertise with the local NPR station and, true to brand form, created some campy and cheeky ads that conveyed his playful perspective. His strongest marketing tools are word of mouth and turning new customers into loyal returning patrons. "Sometimes, the best testament of our brand value is when people find a bug in their food and are good-natured about us replacing it. They really admire that you walk your talk and provide pesticide-free food right from the source!"

Brand is Not Just a Logo: It's Everything

From this authentic core, your brand can spring forth. Once you acknowledge how you change people's lives—whether you sell to consumers or to other businesses—you can better understand how to convey that across all of your communications. When I say communications, I mean **every touchpoint you have with people—visual, verbal, and experiential.** Customers see your brand in the visual elements you convey: your logo, website, packaging, and signage. They hear your brand in your website copy, live presentations, elevator pitch, and press stories. And they experience your brand through the buying process, how they're treated by customer service, the caliber of your employees, and so on.

Let's take an example. Suppose you sell chic, simple humidors for cigar aficionados. Your ideal customer is someone—perhaps a woman—who loves cigars but doesn't want the humidor to stick out like a sore thumb in her home. Most humidors are bulky and showy objects made of dark, heavy wood. But a whole client base out there likes simple, clean lines in their homes and wants something to go with their décor. The problem you solve for them is to make cigars fit unobtrusively into their stylish homes and lifestyle. "Simple. Clean. Unobtrusive. Chic."

Given this, would you ever design a website with cramped copy, minimal white space, and a confusing array of choices? Would your logo be loud and bold to get noticed? Would your customer service reps sound harried and rushed when answering the phone?

No, no, and no. Your site might be simple to navigate and your colors would represent simple elegance and sophistication, perhaps using white, silver, and black as a contrast to competitors' dark, heavy colors. For your products, you'd show basic color and design options and simple shots of each, with a short description. Your copy tone would be refined and casual—not based on hyperbole and exclamation points. Your call center reps would be courteous, to the point, and knowledgeable. They would efficiently take care of customers without noise or chaos in the background.

This is what it means to live your brand in everything you do. Now every time a customer comes to your website, sees your product, encounters your ads, or calls your sales order line, they have a consistent experience. When you extend your brand beyond the promotional or visual aspects to include policies, hiring decisions, or the like, I call this **operationalizing your brand.** You inject the brand into the DNA of your company and ensure the entire customer experience is clear and consistent. And this "brands" (pun intended) you into their psyche to occupy the "simple, chic, unobtrusive, clean" space in their brain.

See how much easier all the other decisions become when you know who you are and what you're about? If you don't have a solid brand foundation, your decisions will be random and end up costing you money for nothing.

Brand as Design Guide: Hug a Designer Today

People tend to think designers are magical wizards who can read minds and create intricate, beautiful visuals within an hour. Eager entrepreneurs with hope in their eyes seek out designers to turn visions into reality. They plead, "Make me a logo" or "Build me a website," but offer no direction as to what these items should communicate.

Going to a designer for a logo and website without a Brand Strategy is like handing someone a wad of money and saying, "Go shopping." If you don't say what you need, for whom you're buying, and for what occasion, only a mind reader would be able to accurately spend that money on what you desire. If you treat a designer this casually, I can see countless revisions and billable hours in your future.

This is an extreme example for effect, but it's what people often do when working with designers. We ask them to communicate something visually without a clear directive on what we want to communicate and to whom. Or we give them our personal taste: "I love pink" or "I want my logo to be a cat, because I like cats." This is all well and good—and the fun part of owning your own business—but if you haven't thought about your audience and what they want and need, you'll have the prettiest website at the party but no one will ask you to dance. Your designer will struggle to visually convey what you're trying to communicate, which will be frustrating to both of you. It's sound business practice to not just hire a good agency, but to be a good client as well.

If you want a funny tagline on your logo, is that because it will resonate with your audience or you personally just like funny taglines? But what if you're a funeral home?

If you're selling to teenagers, should you have a traditional, boring website? Aha! Don't make a false assumption and say no right off the bat. Maybe you do need a simple site. The layout depends on the teens you're trying to attract, what brand promise you offer, and what they need.

Know thy brand, know thy audience: only then can your designer easily create thy logo, website, and brochures. You will also know how to package your products, how to answer the phone, and what your automated e-mail from customer service should say. Any writer you hire can also more easily craft your main messages and tagline.

Bridget Perez, a partner at TRAY Creative (TRAYcreative. com) is a creative director who helps businesses communicate their brand visually and ensure the designs impact the buying decision. In her experience, color is one of the most important elements of branding. "Sixty percent of the decision to buy a product is based on color," she says. "The brain registers shape first, then color, then content when recognizing or remembering something, like a logo. Think about a well-known brand, like Target or UPS, then imagine if you saw the Target logo in blue or a UPS truck that was orange . . . would you even register it?" Design choices like color, layout, and font can compel the right audience to buy when they are used correctly—or repel your audience from buying when they are not.

We'll explore more about how to apply color in Part 3.

Part 2:
How to Build Your Brand Strategy

IF YOU HAVE MILLIONS OF DOLLARS and tons of time, you can spend months working with a slick agency to craft your Brand Strategy. They can do primary and secondary research, engage in detailed competitive audits, and test all kinds of concepts. But most small business owners or nonprofit organizations don't have this kind of money or time. You just need a simple strategy to ensure you're on the right path and thinking about the right things.

The ten questions in this section will help you reach the heart of your Brand Strategy.

This process is especially designed for small businesses or startup organizations that lack big budgets.

Two caveats:

One, this book won't tell you the "right" Brand Strategy for your business. As mentioned in Part 1, you need to discover which brand will be most effective for *your* target customers, as well as the brand promise you can authentically make and consistently deliver to them. The questions will guide you toward personal answers that fit your organization. If you are a service business or nonprofit agency—just think of "clients" or "donors" instead of "customers".

Two, the answers to the ten questions aren't meant to be the exact words you'll use for marketing materials. Your answers will be raw materials you can later shape into website copy, a brochure, or even store signage. Without this internal foundation, you won't even know how to start writing those external messages.

Your answers will form the basis of your Brand Strategy. The information you glean from this exercise will save time, money, and frustration on a thousand little business decisions. And if you share these ten answers with a designer or writer, be prepared: they may jump up and hug you. Many such professionals build time into their project costs to go over these steps with you, so if you can do this heavy lifting on your own—and I believe you can—then you'll save time and money.

You may need to hire a writer for a few hours to help polish your ideas, but you'll already have the bulk of your strategy done. This will be your first step to ensuring the clarity and consistency we talked about in Part 1.

In addition, don't worry about format. Answer these questions however you wish. You can use Word, Excel, or PowerPoint. You might even try the old-fashioned way by writing things down in a notebook. In this exercise, your thought process is much more important than format.

The Ten Key Questions to Building Your Brand Strategy

1. How do you describe your organization and what you do?

2. What are the products or services and how are they packaged and priced?

3. What are your strengths and weaknesses?

4. What are the adjectives and emotions around your brand?

5. Who and where is your ideal audience?

6. What are the main customer benefits and why do they matter? Why can you make those claims?

7. Who is your competition and how are you different?

8. How do you need to communicate with customers and prospects?

9. What is your organization's one greatest asset?

10. How do we measure success?

Question 1: How do you describe your organization and what you do?

Small businesses and start-ups often try to run before they can walk by dazzling the public with lofty marketing-speak, leaving folks asking, "What is it you actually *do?*" If you can't condense the essence of what you do into one or two crisp sentences, you won't be able to create benefit statements and other brand elements later on. I'd be a millionaire by now if I had a dollar for every time someone at a networking event gets up to talk about their small business, but never bothers clarifying whether they sell a product or a service, or if they operate online versus just a brick-and-mortar establishment.

What does your business or organization do? Forget the marketing gloss. When it comes right down to it, what product or service do you provide to whom and why should they care?

Before we move on to loftier things like a mission statement or a tagline, you need to have this basic description down cold. A mighty oak starts as a tiny acorn.

> Before we move on to loftier things like a mission statement or a tagline, you need to have the basic description of "What You Do" down cold.

Seems simple, right? But have you ever talked to two employees of the same organization who describe the business in totally different ways? Drives me crazy, too. I find this step is often the most powerful way to clear away the clutter, and it builds a strong brand and messaging base. Just as basketball players start with the fundamentals before they can be the next Michael Jordan, you've got to nail the simple drills before you can tackle the complex plays.

Are you a product or service? Are you a content provider or distributor? Are you only online or do you have a physical shop?

Do you plan events or connect people at events? Do you resell a manufacturer's product or make your own? Do you sell wholesale or direct to consumers? You should be able to boil this down to one or two sentences. Here are some examples:

- A manufacturer of athletic footwear, apparel, and equipment for men, women and children
- A provider of women's hair care products and services, online and through salons
- A maker of automobile windows and windshields
- A programmer for small business websites
- A business coach who helps entrepreneurs write business plans
- A nonprofit agency that provides shelter, resources, and job training to the homeless in urban areas

Leave the branding stuff—pithy taglines or the "we guide women down the right path" mission statements—for later. Don't start with such tactical marketing-speak before you build the Brand Strategy to support those messages. Later on, your tactics will include creating all the necessary customer-facing copy.

Another way to approach this question in its simplest form is to adopt the approach of Christopher Flett, founder of Ghost CEO (Ghostceo.com) and author of *What Men Don't Tell Women About Business* (Wiley). Ghost CEO provides leadership development training and business consulting to women business owners. I love Chris's pragmatic, take-no-prisoners style as he helps businesswomen attain success. Chris and his team always ask clients, right off the bat, to describe their business in the following way: "What do you do? Why does it matter? Who cares?" That's it, bottom line. No catch phrases or taglines. Everything else is built upon how clearly you answer these questions.

> ## EXERCISE:
>
> Write a basic description of what your organization does and who it serves in an easy-to-understand sentence or two, with no marketing hype. Run this by a few people who know nothing about your business and see if they get what you do and for whom you do it.

Question 2: What are the products or services and how are they packaged and priced?

Even if they haven't started their business yet, most people have a good idea of what products or services they want to offer and at what price. If you're a writer, do you charge by the hour, by the project, or do you offer a Communication Basics Package that includes five pages of website copy, a company description, press release boilerplate, and a tagline—all for one price? If you're a boutique, do you sell certain products within a given price range? You may need to pull some of this information from your business plan.

We answer this question in a more abstract way than you would on a detailed revenue forecasting model. Why? Because we have a different purpose in mind: brand development. This process assumes the prices you offer have already been vetted within a forecasting model or business-planning process and that you aren't losing money on each sale.

I recommend you save the answers to this question, because later on you'll perform a sanity check against the rest of your Brand Strategy. For example, if you go through the entire Brand Strategy process and find your target audience is small business owners, you'll want to be sure your price points are reasonable for this audience, versus an audience of multimillion dollar corporations. Or you may find, as some of my clients have, that you *want* to target a certain audience, but you've priced your products or services way out of their reach.

You also need to include pricing in your Brand Strategy because it will eventually contribute to *how* you represent your brand. Will you be the Porsche of your industry? If so, you may need to increase your prices to align with this brand promise. Otherwise, people won't believe in your value. Or do you want to be the Kia of your market? If so, high prices don't align with that image and the target audience who would buy the Kia can't afford you. What good does it do if all of your customer touchpoints are talking to folks who can't buy from you? You either need to change your prices or alter your brand image. You could position yourself as "Porsche quality at Kia prices," but then you'd have to deliver on that promise—and you might not be bringing in enough revenue to realistically fulfill this for customers, thus leaving a bad taste in their mouths.

In addition, writing down the actual packages or items you offer will help you compare apples to apples when you examine the competition. For example, you might be the only one who offers a unique package in your market. That's a company strength you'll want to emphasize at the end when we put the brand into action in Part 3 of this book.

EXERCISE:

In a table or grid, list each product or service you offer and how much you charge. If you offer packages, note these and write down everything they include. If you're a retail shop or online store with many items, list a representative sample of items and the price ranges for each. For example, a boutique might offer "Casual dresses, ranging from $200 to $500; Jewelry, ranging from $50 to $400."

Question 3: What are your strengths and weaknesses?

Your brand communications should ideally play to your strengths and downplay or address your weaknesses, turning them into positives. By strengths and weaknesses, I'm not referring to your individual products. I'm talking about your business as a whole. Since this is your corporate Brand Strategy, we need to take the macro view on this answer rather than considering individual products. The answers will form the basis of the words you use and the company's overall visual look and feel. You can certainly talk in the aggregate about your product offering ("We're the only distributor of Product X in the region") but avoid a laundry list of specific product strengths and weaknesses. Remember, this exercise will help you focus on overall businesses strengths you want to convey with your company's brand.

What does your business really have going for it? Where is your business vulnerable?

What does your business really have going for it? What unique things can your business offer? What compelling assets, skills, or connections do you have? Where is your business vulnerable? Where do you fall down against the competition? You may find some of these answers in your business plan. As a small business owner or founder, you may represent the face of your business: your personal strengths are its strengths. So, a strength can even be YOU. For example, being well-connected in the community gives you an advantage over other businesses. Or do you have unique experience in your background that no one in your space can claim, making you an expert?

In the next Brand at Work case study, we see how one woman's unique professional background is her main brand strength and, by communicating it throughout her company's messages and operations, helps her business stand out.

//

Brand at Work: Major Mom

Who better to get your home or office in tip-top order than a former U.S. Air Force Major? That unique brand differentiator helps Angela Cody-Rouget, CPO (chief professional organizer) of Major Mom (MajorMom.biz) stand out from hundreds of bland, look-alike professional organizing companies. Major Mom's brand promise is to make organizing fun and to get the job done faster than anyone. And Angela walks her talk. She has two decades of training in order management, serving in the U.S. Air Force for eighteen years and eventually attaining the rank of major. She embraces and thrives in orderly environments. The company's mission is "to restore order and serenity to a client's home and office so they will experience the joy of living and working in organized and beautifully arranged environments." The mission is bigger than just "putting stuff away." Angela is out to restore peace in the home and bring families together.

This efficient and professional brand promise is the basis for every decision—from employees' unique camo and T-shirt uniforms to an efficient hiring process mapped out on their website. "Each time we create forms to use on the job or train our staff, we're thinking about brand consistency," Angela says. "We create our HR, PR, Client Care, Marketing and Sales Systems with our brand in mind. Consistency will help us build a national company."

Running her company like a well-oiled machine assures clients that Angela can indeed get their own homes and offices in order. This consistency is further articulated in a new-recruit training academy and six-month apprenticeship that ensures all Major Mom Liberators (not just Angela) will adopt and live the brand values.

Angela's distinct mission, vision, and brand values are clearly and consistently communicated across every brochure, ad, website page, and even their voicemail message. These values consciously guide business decisions. In one case, Angela turned down a PR opportunity on an influential radio and TV personality's show because his approach and demeanor didn't align with Major Mom's brand and values. She has also turned down a partnership opportunity with another organizing company that focused on "hauling junk" rather than her mission of making your home your treasure. Having such a strong brand that breaks the mold enabled Angela to extend beyond Colorado to Arizona. She's well on her way to achieving her vision to be the most recognized and respected organizing firm in the United States and the world.

A weakness could be "It's a crowded market of many look-alikes" or "I lack start-up capital so I have to charge up front for services." Be honest with yourself. Being modest might cause you to miss a valuable opportunity to emphasize the good things and downplay the bad.

Many start-ups could stand to spend a day with key corporate stakeholders, or even a select group of their customers, to figure out what makes them tick and how they could improve. If you're an established business with customers, ask them what they think. Why did they buy from you? What drew them to you? What do they think you are lacking? Customers are a gold mine of information for businesses. Don't be afraid. Customers who like you will want you to succeed and they won't mind being part of that process. You can further cement your relationship with them by bringing them into this branding process. Send them a quick survey online via Emma (Myemma.com) or SurveyMonkey (Surveymonkey. com) to glean this information. Just remember to ask them to be honest and offer some type of incentive, such as a complimentary service, discount coupon, or a free coffee card, in exchange for their valuable time.

If that's too complicated, then send an email or letter to a select group of customers and ask for their opinion. You might try polling a customer who made a return or bought from you once and never again, just to get juicy feedback. Keep the survey under ten questions to respect their time and try not to ask leading questions like, "Do you like our amazingly low prices that offer real value for the money?" Articles and videos are available on the web to help you craft a good survey—just type "effective surveys" into your favorite online search engine.

I once worked on a Brand Strategy project for a nonprofit organization that wanted to increase donations and community awareness about its services. As part of this work, we interviewed a representative sample of stakeholders, including employees, clients, donors, and board members, to get a sense of their brand perception and what they felt the organization was doing right and wrong. But the nonprofit went a step further and had us interview clients who had a negative experience. This yielded some of the most profound insights and perspectives for us. While happy folks talked about the brand in terms of what the company intended to communicate, the unhappy folks showed us gaps between brand promise and the brand reality.

Because brand lives in the mind of your customers, you need to take some of the bad with the good in order to make improvements. The executive director knew that for every one of these unhappy folks willing to talk, at least ten others had the same viewpoint but didn't speak up—they just walked away. Worse, they virally spread the word about their negative experience.

Finding out why people don't like you can be even more powerful than finding out why they do. Based on such information, we were able to revise their brand messaging and offer operational recommendations about the organization's training, client care, and communication processes that were out of whack with the brand promise they were touting.

Finding out why people don't like you can be even more powerful than finding out why they do.

EXERCISE:

Create a two-column list with one column titled "Strengths" and the other "Weaknesses". Start listing quick bullet points about you and your business at a high level (not product by product) for each column. Got a great location? Dub that a strength. Are you brand new in town and lack a strong community network to promote your business? Make that a weakness. Do you, as the founder or CEO, have a unique educational, work, or personal history that your competitors lack? List that as a strength. If you're small and your competitors are large, this could be a weakness when it comes to buying power and awareness, but it could be a strength: you might be more flexible when working with clients and offer more personalized service. In that case, you'd list your size under both columns.

Question 4: What are the adjectives and emotions around your brand?

This is the fun stuff. If you think at all about brand, this is probably the task that most often comes to mind. The adjectives, images, or emotions around your brand are also known as **brand attributes**. What descriptive words come to mind when you think about your company and its offerings? How do you want others to see you? Decide which space in customers' minds you want to occupy; in which mental file drawer you want them to tuck you away. Do you want to be professional, serious, and trusted, or do you want to be playful and sassy? Do you want to be formal or casual?

Decide which space in customers' minds you want to occupy; in which mental file drawer you want them to tuck you away.

Having these listed will help a designer see your vision and create an appropriate logo or website. And these words will also educate a writer on what tone or word choices are best for your marketing messages and website copy.

You can also leverage the brands of people or characters to describe your own brand attributes. If I describe a brand as Audrey Hepburn, you instantly get a picture of grace, femininity, elegance, and beauty without me saying all of that. So don't be afraid to borrow images from famous people or historical personalities in your Brand Strategy to help convey your vision. I once had a technology client who wanted to be the Anderson Cooper of his niche space: young, tech-savvy, trusted, intelligent, and professional. Analogies are a useful tool to help you judge the fit of a marketing program or to describe what you want your designer to do with your website. Another great way to do this is by comparing your organization to other items that have brands, as we discussed in Part 1: holidays, places, TV shows, movies, or fictional characters. Are you New York City or Santa Fe? *The Deadliest Catch* or *The View?* Romantic comedy or crime thriller?

Small businesses and start-ups tend to list way too many brand attributes, to the point that they can't possibly represent *all* of them. I recommend that clients brainstorm everything that comes to mind first, and then go back and cut that list in half. Then cut it in half again and repeat until they're left with the most crucial five to seven adjectives, images, or phrases. As we stated in Part 1, trying to be everything to everyone will result in being nothing to no one. Focus on what's most important.

This short list may lead to a positioning statement such as, "I want my business to be the Rolls Royce of car washes." You may not end up putting that verbatim description before the public, but it goes a long way toward helping a designer create an appropriate logo or helping you decide whether an ad in a particular magazine might tarnish the brand image you want to convey.

EXERCISE:

Make a list of every adjective, emotion, analogy, character, or genre that best describes what you want your organization to represent. Think about what image you want customers to have of you. Try to pare this list down to five to seven strong points that will help focus your efforts without creating an unattainable image for a designer or writer. If your list is too long, keep cutting it in half until you get to the five to seven most important traits and images.

Brand at Work: Blue Bottle Coffee Co.

Whether you are an in-the-know San Francisco techie or a visiting tourist on the search for great food and drink, you know Blue Bottle Coffee (Bluebottlecoffee.com) Founder and CEO James Freeman, a jaded clarinet player, was super nuts about coffee and roasted it fresh at home. But though he searched high and low back in 2002, he just couldn't find coffee from the standard shops out there with a roast date on it. Tired of pumpkin soy lattes and caramel fudge macchiatos, James was consumed by the idea of a great cup of pure, simple, freshly brewed coffee. Why couldn't the process be more like a farmers market, he lamented, where you give someone money for a handcrafted fresh product? This personal desire for something he loved fueled the passion behind Blue Bottle Coffee.

Originally a local San Francisco farmers market fixture, Blue Bottle's demand was soon so great, he opened a shop in 2005.

Eager customers wait longer than at most coffee spots while their cup is made to order for maximum freshness and flavor. "We hit a nerve with urban-loving people who tend to be more educated about coffee—or would like to be," says James. "People like me, who wanted an alternative. We handcraft delicious coffee, cup by cup, for less than five dollars, so you don't have to be super privileged to come into our shop."

This passion to keep things fresh, pure, and simple plays out in the visual and verbal aspects of the brand. The stripped-down logo of a simple blue bottle is very approachable. Nothing fluffy, nothing extra. James believes good design, like good coffee, is more about what you don't see—what is edited out—so that it remains honest and true. "I never like 'extra stuff,'" says James. "We skip the bells and whistles and just use good coffee beans, water, and time. It's how we make great coffee."

The brand voice follows a similar no-fuss, no-muss philosophy. It's welcoming and not as boyish as many coffee companies tend to be. James calls it "charmingly didactic." No chatter, no slogans, no quotation marks. "You only need to explain yourself and go into detail when it's called for," he says. He doesn't want to *tell* people what their experience should be—he simply wants them to *have it*.

While James eschewed a formal mission statement, the company lives out a brand strategy via three simple tenets that inform everything they do: *Deliciousness, hospitality,* and *sustainability*. "These three words answer all the questions we may have," says James.

"Deliciousness" informs how they make their coffee: One cup at a time using coffee less than 48 hours out of the roaster so it can be enjoyed at its peak of flavor. They only use the finest organic, and pesticide-free, shade-grown beans.

"Hospitality" guides how they treat not just customers but employees and vendors. "Hospitality implies respect for everyone," says James. "Good employee benefits. Paying suppliers on time. Up, down, and sideways, this informs every interaction throughout the company. It's about action, not just words."

Their commitment to sustainability and the environment means using coffee bags lined with polylactic acid (PLA) derived from corn and made from craft paper, which is recyclable or compostable. Most coffee bags consist of plastic and foil layers. Eighty percent of Blue Bottle's coffees are certified organic, as are most of their ingredients such as milk and sugar. And they are rabid about minimizing landfill waste. When a supplier shifted to non-recyclable packaging, James got them on the phone to complain that the move would triple Blue Bottle's landfill waste. The supplier promptly changed back to 100 percent paper. They also encourage sustainability by giving the best possible prices to coffee farmers who follow similar practices.

Blue Bottle's passionate philosophy fuels its success and cult following. They are beloved in social media, specifically Twitter, Facebook, and Instagram. In addition to ten stores (half in the San Francisco Bay Area and half in New York), they boast a small network of cafés, wholesale partners, vintage German coffee roasters, and even an espresso cart. They want to maintain their handcrafted vibe and do not desire to be a global chain with millions of locations.

This brand seems to have brewed the perfect recipe for success.

Question 5: Who and where is your ideal audience?

This is the **single most important aspect to a strong Brand Strategy.** If you don't know your audience intimately and make them real, you'll be shooting at a moving target. Often, business owners say, "Everyone is my target audience." They're afraid to exclude a particular group, because in certain situations, that person *could* feasibly buy something from them. Yes, in the big picture, anyone may buy anything, but you need to focus your attention and dollars on the ones *most likely* to buy. We aren't talking about *to whom you're willing to sell*: we're talking about where you'll spend your limited time and money on attracting the lowest-hanging fruit.

> Think about your *ideal customer,* not your average customer.

Think about your ideal customer, not your average customer. "Average" will dilute your answer too much, leading to generic, vanilla communication that won't appeal to anyone. I always tell clients, "When you try to be everything to everyone, you end up being nothing to nobody." It's akin to throwing a dart at a dartboard that has no bull's-eye in the center, but is painted all white: how will you know where to aim, or if you're even close to the target?

Pretend you have a group of one hundred people in a room and can pick the dream person who best represents your ideal client or customer. Who would that be? Or select an example from your best customers and base the profile on him or her.

For example, you can say you sell to women, but that category is much too broad. Do you mean a grandma or a newlywed? City girl or country girl? Married or single? Parent or not? Working or stay-at-home? There are many different women out there, with different buying needs, interests, and styles. Generally speaking, a progressive twenty-four-year-old single graphic designer in Los

Angeles may have different tastes and needs than a conservative forty-year-old, stay-at-home mother of four in Duluth, Minnesota. Flesh out as much detail for this ideal customer as you can. Give her a name and an occupation. Tell me where she works (if she works), how she gets there, what she reads, what she watches on TV (does she watch TV?), where she shops, how she dresses, and where she gets her news and information. To what clubs or groups does she belong? What does she do for fun? All of this will help later on when you invest in marketing tactics, because you'll be able to see which ideas will get in front of your targets and which are a waste of time and money. It will also help you discover unexpected ways to reach your audience.

A past client in financial services came to work with me on the Brand Strategy for his new business. He had no website, no materials, nothing: this is one of *my* ideal client segments. But he did have a script for a TV ad he'd written and eagerly hoped to use one day. His ad was good, but while going through the ten-step process we discovered his ideal client was too busy balancing her own successful firm and her family to even watch TV. If she did watch, she recorded programs and zapped past the commercials, so investing in a local TV ad would have been a waste of money. By doing the ideal-customer exercise, however, we uncovered a channel he had never thought about: radio. His ideal client commutes to work in her car for at least twenty minutes a day and she most likely listens to NPR. So investing in a radio ad on the local NPR station was much more effective than a local TV spot.

Another client figured out her ideal customer frequents coffee shops more than most people. Even though her business didn't seem to jump out and scream, "Advertise in coffee shops!" she realized well-worded postcards for people to pick up and take back to their offices would be just the thing. They could then log on to her site from the office, or even right at the coffee shop because her ideal customers held meetings there. Unless you do this creative exercise, you may never discover unique little ways to get in front of your best potential customers.

On the flip side, this exercise also helps you avoid spending money on marketing that doesn't work. NASCAR is hugely popular with certain types of people and draws millions to their events, but do you think Nordstrom spends money marketing there to reach its ideal client? Would Harley-Davidson advertise at a tennis match? Knowing your customer intimately will help you avoid the temptation to invest in just any marketing opportunity or partnership that crosses your path. You'll have a perfect benchmark to judge the worth of advertising campaigns.

Many clients are afraid to eliminate a potential group of customers. They say, "But I could sell to this person, or this person, or that person. And one time, this one type of customer did buy from me, so maybe I should be marketing to that whole segment. I can't leave any of them out because they're all potential sales." The reality is that you only have so much money to spend and so much time. You want to go deep on the activities that get the most traction, not pursue a broad range of one-time activities that get you nowhere. The broad range approach is akin to skipping a stone over water: you'll hit a lot of points, but won't make a big impression in any of them.

Don't be afraid of this exercise—you'll end up catching ancillary people in your net even if you don't target them, and it's not like you won't take their money if they don't fit your ideal customer criteria. This is not about to whom you will sell (although if you are a service business, it could serve as a great checklist for determining which clients you will or will not take on). This is about deciding where to focus your time, energy, and budget for the greatest impact. Think of it as a fashion designer does: who will be your "brand muse"?

In the following Brand at Work case study, you can see how CasaQ carved out a unique focus instead of trying to do it all—and how this specific expertise has made them a sought-after partner.

\\

Brand at Work: CasaQ

Darlene Tenes used to sell imported décor items from Mexico. But when she wanted to find home products with a Latino flair, there was nothing on the market or at gift shows that met her quality and authenticity standards. Sensing a need, Darlene decided to design culturally significant products herself that reflected her own lifestyle and values.

She created CasaQ (Casaq.com), a San Jose, California-based, Hispanic lifestyle company dedicated to providing unique products, services, and content geared toward people who embrace the Latino culture. CasaQ is focused on inspiring others to learn, teach, and share this rich culture. "I am very particular about getting the details of the designs and the history correct on all of my products," Darlene says.

CasaQ could go beyond Latino-inspired products but Darlene stays true to her core brand promise, which ends up resonating with folks outside that demographic. "CasaQ is about sharing and preserving our culture and in doing so, it creates a bond with other people who have similar traditions and customs, many of which have been shared or merged with other cultures." Forty percent of their retail sales and 90 percent of their wholesale buyers are not Latino.

CasaQ is based on the things Darlene authentically finds most important in life: faith, culture, family, and of course, food. The "Q" stands for *querida* which means "loving" or "darling." And *Casa Querida* means "a loving home," which is exactly what she has in mind when designing her ornaments. Simply using the Q in the company name helps the company remain memorable to non-Spanish speakers and thus easier to find online.

This loving-home brand value extends to treating customers like family. They gladly replace or refund broken items, no questions asked. And if CasaQ makes an order mistake, they send a handwritten note and small gift. "My employees need to have a passion for history and culture so they can be excited about the products and mission of the company no matter what their position. That's part of being a team or a family," says Darlene.

Living this brand mission inside and out has helped CasaQ attract some big accounts. Grupo Modelo, the manufacturers of Corona and Modelo beers, approached the company because of their focus and understanding of Latino culture. "Other ornament manufacturers may have slapped their logo on an ornament or created a copy of the beer bottle but it wasn't in our DNA to do so," says Darlene. "I personally sketched and designed ornaments that celebrated popular icons in the Latino culture and incorporating their logo into such designs as a Mexican Luchador and Loteria cards."

That focus and passion for the culture has helped CasaQ get into major museums, exclusive gift stores, and even Macy's and Fab.com because buyers trust the knowledge and care that is put into each product. Next up: a line of kitchen textile products will be added to the collection.

My husband is another great example of catching others outside of your ideal customer in your net. He's an avid video gamer, and we own a Wii, a PSP, and an XBOX. He is in his late-thirties, and is a successful tech-company executive with a wife, a mortgage, and a dog. Do you really think the XBOX team is spending money and time specifically trying to reach his target profile? Probably not. They're going after younger, single guys who have fewer obligations and more gaming time. In fact, I see their ads on TV networks that target that specific demographic. But this doesn't mean their messages don't resonate with someone like my husband. After all, he watches those networks occasionally, right?

He still gets caught in the net because the products and brand promise appeal to him. Will XBOX video games specifically devote dollars and time to reaching a whole segment of people like my husband? Maybe, if they get enough traction from it (and from recent marketing, it now appears the brand does target adult males like my husband as a unique customer profile.) But the more important point is that such ideal-customer profiles guide the company on where and how to target their brand and marketing dollars. If they catch others in that net, that's just gravy.

Companies the size of Microsoft use different customer profiles for each product group. They sell both consumer and business products, after all, and *every* brand and product in their portfolio doesn't appeal to *every* audience type.

A few years ago, I read that Hyundai was creating a line of cars especially for folks who are moving back to the city from the suburbs. According to the article, "Their ideal customer is a couple in their late fifties who have traded in their sprawling suburban home for a nicely appointed condo in an up-and-coming city, like Seattle. They have sold off one of their two cars and are decluttering their lives. They socialize, eat well, and live for new experiences."[11]

Now, many of these traits have nothing to do with buying a car, and I'm sure if someone in their twenties who doesn't eat well and lives with mom and dad wanted to buy a car, Hyundai would still sell one to him. The point is that even companies with millions to spend on marketing and branding do this ideal customer exercise.

Defining your ideal audience also helps with pricing and packaging (Question 3), as we previously stated. You can ensure that what you offer and how you price it is consistent with your ideal customer. You'd be surprised how often the two do not match up initially. For example, saying your ideal customer is a "solopreneur" but then pricing your products too high for his limited budget.

As you learn more and more about your customers, you may find they are not who you initially thought they were. That's okay.

You need to start somewhere. We'll talk more about customer feedback in Part 3 of the book.

EXERCISE:

Write a one-page character profile of your ideal customer in each customer segment which you serve. Try not to create more than three different segments/profiles for now. Give this person a name, an age, and a marital status. Tell me where they work, what they watch on TV, what they do for fun, how much money they make, what a typical day is like for them, how do they commute, which groups or associations they belong to, what magazines they read, and anything else that comes to mind. Be as specific and creative as possible. This will help you see new ways to get your brand in front of the people who matter most.

Question 6: What are the main customer benefits and why do they matter? Why can you make those claims?

Here's a common challenge for small businesses and start-up firms: They often become so involved with daily operations that they only think about what they're selling. They're unable to look at their business with fresh eyes, from a customer's viewpoint. When asked what benefit they provide or why someone should buy from them, they fall back on a product or service description. "The benefit is that we build websites cheaply," or "we sell organic yoga clothes." But how does the customer see you? What value do they receive from using your services or purchasing items from your firm? What problem do they have that your product or service solves?

A simple exercise will help you decide if you've landed on the benefit. Name a feature of your company and ask yourself: "So why does that matter?" If you can keep drilling down and asking, "So what?" then you know you haven't reached the benefit yet.

Here's an example:

"*We sell yoga clothes made from organic materials.*" (So why should organic materials matter to me?)

"*Because the clothes are made of natural, breathable fibers.*" (So why do natural, breathable fibers matter to me?)

"*Because you get more freedom and comfort so you can get the most from your yoga practice.*" (Bingo!)

See how I went from talking about "What We Do" to "What the Clothes Do" to finally "What you—the customer—get"? Many businesses simply tout *what they sell* (features) but don't explain *why anyone should care* (benefits).

Ideally, your features serve as proof for why you can make a certain benefit claim. For example, "side-impact air bags" is a feature; "keeps you safe in a crash" is the benefit. If you're a yoga studio, "We offer five types of yoga classes for all levels" is a feature; "Find just the right class that fits your skill level so you get more out of each class" is the benefit.

If you don't have a good handle on how to verbalize the benefits you provide, you won't be able to build a brand that resonates both consciously and subconsciously with customers. They won't form an attachment to you as a way to make their lives better. The lack of benefits will leave all your marketing messages flat.

Here's a marketing secret: as buyers, we're all selfish beings. Why shouldn't we be? After all, we're spending *our* money. So I ask, "What's in it for me? What does your product or service do for me and why should I believe you?"

In marketing terms, the answers to "What does your product or service do for me?" yield *benefits*. The answers to "Why should I believe you?" yield *proof points* or *features*.

> In marketing terms, the answers to "What does your product or service do for me?" yield *benefits*. The answers to "Why should I believe you?" yield *proof points or features*.

This is true whether you sell to consumers or businesses. Many B2B (business-to-business) technology start-ups revert to spewing out a laundry list of features and functions when trying to make sales. They wonder why this doesn't work. They say, "Showing more features proves to the prospect that our product is way ahead of the competition." But that isn't how it works. You may have the best widgets in the world, but if I can't understand how your product solves my problem, then I just don't care. The features are only proof points that should support a greater benefit. What does the state-of-the-art, advanced widget-producing technology with customized interfaces and nine hundred gigs of cloud-computing space actually *do* for me or my company? How will it solve my problems? Yes, a technical buyer will care about what's behind the curtain (the features), but only *after* he's hooked by what he'll get out of the product overall. And besides, if his job is riding on the decision he makes, one of the benefits could be that he'll look like a rock star and get promoted for choosing your safe, reliable, fast-performing product.

On the flip side of just listing proof points or features, some small businesses tout benefits without proof points. This is useless, because no one will believe your claims. As you build a brand promise you must be able to back it up. Benefits like "low cost" and "best quality" are generic, and you absolutely must prove why you're able to say this. Making the claim isn't enough to build a strong brand in the customer's mind. You'll have to fulfill the brand promise, after all. Remember, brand isn't just what you say it is or what your visuals show; it's how the customer's actual experience aligns with that promise.

Another way to work out the benefits customers get from your products or services is to uncover their problems first and then focus on how your business solves them. You can offer them a vision for what their lives can be like if they have your product or service so they will want to learn more. "Too many companies describe their products to customers by explaining features, "says Matt Heinz of Heinz Marketing (Heinzmarketing.com), a consulting agency that helps businesses with their sales and go-to-market strategies. "That's a mistake, especially at the front of the conversation and sales cycle. To gain the customer's attention, you have to speak in terms of benefits. Don't talk about the *how* and *what*. Address the *why*."

Let's take an example. Joe's firm offers customers new websites built on the WordPress platform, or he transitions HTML-based websites over to this platform. This is what he does or sells (Question 1). But the *benefit* Joe provides is a low-cost way to get a high-quality website. He solves the customer dilemma that "good websites cost too much to build and maintain." Joe has a few proof points (or features) to back up this low-cost claim: One, he works remotely from his home office, giving him low overhead. Two, he uses pre-built templates and customizes them, rather than spending hours coding new sites from scratch. And three, Joe uses WordPress, an easy-to-use website platform, so his customers can update the sites on their own, rather than paying a programmer to make changes. Joe's high-quality proof points are that he personally customizes each website until it's exactly what the client wants, and the templates he uses are the best WordPress has to offer in terms of flexibility and support.

Why should people buy from you? What problem do you solve? Why should they care or believe you? The answers to this step form the basis of a full-blown messaging platform, and they'll help you create the elevator pitch you'll learn more about in Part 3 of the book.

EXERCISE:

Compose a list of three to five main benefits your business provides, from a customer's point of view. Think about what customers ultimately gain by using your products or services. Do you increase their profits, lower their costs, make them more beautiful, boost self-confidence, preserve precious memories, or reduce stress?

For each main benefit, create a bulleted list of three proof points that show why you can make that claim. Try to be concise with your language—don't ramble on for multiple sentences about each benefit.

Question 7: Who is your competition and how are you different?

Creating a snapshot of your competition and the reasons people might buy from them is always a smart move. This way, your brand promise and messaging can clearly address how you're different and why customers should come to you instead. Many business owners can verbally explain to me why they're a better alternative than the competition, but that information doesn't come across clearly in their messaging or the brand itself. Branding is all about differentiating your business from the other options customers have. This question seems easy if business owners have a direct competitor. But I challenge you to think of competition in a broader sense, as your customers might. What else competes for the dollars they might spend with you? If you're a website designer, then competition is more than just other designers; it could be hosting services that offer DIY templates and website authoring tools (i.e., GoDaddy).

In the software industry, the biggest competitor may not be another software firm offering the exact same solution, but a customer who opts to build their own custom solution in-house from scratch rather than buy a packaged product. This is also known as *Build vs. Buy.*

Other competition might be internal priorities that compete for the money a customer might spend on your product or service. Knowing what you're up against will help you craft messaging that speaks directly to this issue and enables you to say why you're the best alternative or the best use of the budget dollars.

> Knowing what you're up against will help you craft messaging that speaks directly to this issue and enables you to say why you're the best alternative or the best use of the budget dollars.

Competition can be seasonal as well. Pretend you own a flower shop. Yes, your competitors are other florists in the area, but what about during the days leading up to Valentine's Day or Mother's Day? During those times, a florist might be competing with other unique businesses who are also trying to get their hands on the customer's discretionary funds. Rick, for example, knows he's going to buy something for his wife on Valentine's Day. He has a pool of money set aside for a gift. Rick could choose to spend that money with you, the florist, or he could go to the chocolate shop or the jewelry store. For those special events, several other business types compete with you even though you don't offer the same products. Normally, if someone wants chocolate, they aren't going to look for it in a flower shop or jewelry store, so these businesses aren't always in competition. But during Valentine's Day season, any place that Rick can spend the money he set aside is now your competition. If you want Rick to shop with you, find a way to communicate why your flowers are the best gift choice.

> **EXERCISE:**
>
> Create a list of your competitors, including direct competition and the indirect competition mentioned above. For each competitor, list bullet points of what they provide. Be brief. Then, list why you're a better alternative and how what you offer is different. For this exercise, we can start to look back on the other questions we've answered so far, such as benefits and strengths. You may find those items are also differentiators for you to tout, vis-à-vis your competition. Knowing how to clearly position yourself against your competitors will help you craft messaging *and* create a visual brand identity that separates you from the pack, like it did for Intersource LLC in the following Brand at Work case study.

Brand at Work: Intersource LLC

Technology consulting firms often appear similar, using the same meaningless jargon like "best-of-breed solutions" or "maximize ROI." How can a firm with a unique approach and steadfast values stand out from the competition? Jack Leary, CEO and founder of Intersource LLC (Intersourcellc.com) in Seattle, Washington, knew from the start that the firm he built was different from the rest. He just needed a way to articulate that difference to his prospective target market: innovative companies looking to change, challenge the status quo, and offer amazing products and services.

"In every project, we've delivered success based on not just what we do, but who we are: committed, experienced, honor-bound people," says Jack. "We measure success by our level of impact—period. It's not about overpromising, staffing sub-par resources to save money, or making clients pay for things they don't need. But I knew we were being lumped into the same old 'staffing shops' that simply offer interchangeable consultants who often lack the right experience."

Jack worked with Red Slice to articulate messaging that made their brand stand out and convey the unique principles on which he founded Intersource. The result was a technology consulting firm with a voice unlike any other: frank, honest, jargon-free and—on occasion—a bit cheeky. A website visit instantly shows prospects and customers that they are dealing with a different type of firm: one where "straight talk meets straight tech" to get you where you want to go. Minimal color and fluff, combined with bold typography choices, further demonstrate the firm's commitment to a straightforward experience.

"We wanted people to know that our expert consultants don't hide behind fancy words or trite methodologies. Doing this through approachable language and an uncluttered site helps them immediately trust us to solve their market-changing challenges efficiently, honestly, and creatively."

Jack, a former lieutenant commander in the U.S. Navy, felt strongly about conveying the firm's values up-front: honesty, integrity, discipline, wisdom, and creative thinking. The messaging is hard for competitors to copy because it is authentic to his personal values, which are now woven into Intersource's own brand fabric. More than just words, the values convey the very manner in which the company partners with clients. They are one of the few technology consultancies with such a "Philosophy" page on their website and these values inform everything from how they hire to how they speak.

Intersource's brand messaging is written to sound like you are talking directly to the man who started it all. No gimmicks. No facades. Just honor, integrity, results, and a bit of wit. And that's just the way Jack Leary likes it.[12]

Question 8: How do you need to communicate with customers and prospects?

If you're starting a business from scratch, this one might be a bit loose at the beginning, but remember the Brand Strategy is a living document you can refer back to over time and continue to update. For those of you who already have a business up and running, how are you communicating with your audiences? If your answer is "I'm not really sure," then you already know you have a problem. Branding is about a two-way communication with your customers. If you have no way to talk to them, and more importantly, listen to them, your brand will never grab their loyalty.

You may have answers like "our website" or "marketing postcards." That's okay—list every communication vehicle you have with them, even if it is one-way communication. List your ads, events, catalogs, press releases—all of these are communication vehicles. But also list things like e-newsletters, blogs, automatic email order confirmations, and Twitter if those are mechanisms you use. All your "people interactions" are communication vehicles as well as branding opportunities: store clerks, call center representatives, and your office receptionist.

Now, you can go back to your ideal-audience profile and compare notes. How *should* you be communicating with them? Where are they, what information do they need, and which vehicles do they prefer? Which vehicles will they actually pay attention to? Are you spending countless hours on Twitter right now, but your ideal-customer profile says your best customers don't even use Twitter? Do you mail an expensive printed newsletter each month, but your customers prefer to get all their communication via email? Do your customers even need a newsletter? This step is important, because you need to consciously compare your communication vehicles with your ideal audience's needs and habits and see if they fit together. Many business owners and start-ups just go out, guns blazing, with a laundry list of tactics. They say, "I need a blog, I need a Facebook fan page," without stopping to think if this is the best use of their time and money. Not every business needs a blog or a newsletter. Why would you spend time and money on communication vehicles that get you nowhere?

As for acquiring new customers, how can you reach prospects that aren't in your database? Take notice if you're treating existing customers and new prospects as one homogenous audience group—they are not.

> Take notice if you're treating existing customers and new prospects as one homogenous audience group—they are not.

Sometimes business owners decide to launch customer acquisition programs to a list that includes existing customers. That doesn't make sense, does it? Existing customers and new customers have different needs and a different relationship with you. One group knows you exist and has experienced your brand; the other may not have any clue who you are. So try and treat these groups as two separate audiences. Many brand elements will apply to both, like your visual identity or your product quality, for example. But maybe you need two sections on your website with different benefits and messages: one for existing customers and one for newcomers. Maybe a discount offer will work for happy, existing customers to get them to purchase again, but you might need a free trial for new customers so they can get a taste of your products. Again, go back to your ideal-customer profile.

This question also helps you see if too much of your communication is one-way. What mechanisms do you need to put in place for customers to interact with you, offer feedback, or tell you what they want?

What mechanisms do you need to put in place for customers to interact with you, offer feedback, or tell you what they want?

Are you delivering any surveys with incentives for folks to respond back? Are you effectively building a tribe or interactive community that can get word-of-mouth going for you? This is where social media can be very helpful—but again, only if your ideal customer is engaged with social media. Otherwise, it's a waste of time.

EXERCISE:

Create two columns and list all communication vehicles to existing customers on one side, and all vehicles to new prospects on the other. Consider things like ads, website copy, flyers, newsletters, events, and the like. See if there's 100 percent overlap—this may mean you're lumping current customers and prospects together instead of communicating relevant messages to each group. Compare this list back against your ideal-customer profile to ensure these vehicles are the best ways to get in front of them, or if you need an alternative plan.

Question 9: What is your organization's one greatest asset?

We've talked a lot about benefits and differentiators in the steps above. Many small businesses and start-ups often have at least one differentiator or asset that no other competitor can claim.

Many small businesses and start-ups often have at least one differen-tiator or asset that no other competitor can claim.

This unique asset rises to the top in terms of customer importance and the ability to distance from the pack. This could be something you keep coming back to over and over. If so, you want to identify it and hang your brand's hat on it, visually and verbally. What is that one thing that sets you apart? Go back to your strengths and weaknesses or your competitive differentiators and see if one thing uniquely defines you above all else.

For some small businesses, proprietary technology enables customers to do something in a way no one else can. Another business might be the only distributor of a certain top-quality wine within the region. Still others might offer the greatest product selection under the sun in their category—and if they don't have what you're looking for in-store, they can find it for you anywhere in the world. Finally, your greatest asset could be you. If you, as the founder, have a unique set of educational qualifications or life experiences, that could be what sets you apart and what you'll want to emphasize with visual and verbal branding.

A client of mine, Andrea Rae of Alinga Bodywork (Alingabodywork.com), is a massage therapist and energy worker. Dozens of therapists in the Seattle area talk about the same things: serenity, relaxation, and pampering. But Andrea is an outspoken Australian who was an occupational therapist for years, giving her a strong grounding in modern medicine and physical therapy. Her traditional work experience, combined with her pragmatic personality and open mind, give her a unique brand. Her work focuses on delivering results and getting people unstuck physically and mentally, not just on feeling good. So, in her branding we play up her Australian personality and her pragmatic approach of "pampering with purpose." Her background, both educational and personal, is the single most important differentiator she brings to the table. It makes her stand out from everyone else who's selling the same thing. This brand promise yielded a new tagline as well as a newly designed visual identity based on earthy, grounded colors, Aboriginal art, and her sassy personality.

If you can't boil your single greatest asset down to one thing no one else can say, you need to put more thought into your positioning, your product mix, or your audience.

EXERCISE:

Review your strengths and your competitive differentiators from the previous questions, as well as your customer benefits. Write down the single greatest asset of your business. What is the top item that will put your offerings in a unique market position? What is the one claim no one else can make in your market space? What unique asset benefits your customers the most and helps you stand out?

Brand at Work: Taylor Stitch

In 2009, Michael Maher, Barrett Purdum and Michael Armenta started Taylor Stitch (TaylorStitch.com) on a funky street in San Francisco's Mission District. Their dream? To create rugged, refined and practical clothing for men (and now women) by hand. The company aims to modernize staple clothing pieces for men and women by delivering great quality at a reasonable price with impeccable service.

Taylor Stitch's greatest asset is that their clothes are crafted by hand, with quality and love, and that personal attention guides every brand move. "It's a human-run business," says Maher. "Our main goal when we started was to offer a uniquely personal retail experience to make our customers happy." They empower everyone in the organization to delight the customer. Items are made by hand and sent by hand. When mistakes are made, the human touch prevails. "We understand that in a hand-crafted business, mistakes will be made. A shipment might be sent to the wrong person or a loose thread makes it by quality control. On rare occasions this happens, we are up-front with our customers. If we screw up, we're the first to admit it and fix the problem or discount items to make that customer happy. We look at a mistake as an opportunity to create a human connection and a great customer experience."

This emphasis on happiness and humanness impacts hiring as well as the in-store environment. "We hire people who represent the ethos of service that we ourselves believe in, so, no matter whom you encounter in the store, you get a consistent experience that lives up to the brand." Taylor Stitch also pays attention to all five senses when it comes to customer touchpoints: the types of pictures they use, the words they write, the store's music and scents. "We come at retail from a hospitality perspective, not just a product perspective. We believe people don't like to shop if they are uncomfortable, so we created something much more approachable," says Maher.

No matter how large the business grows, Taylor Stitch is committed to maintaining that comfortable "neighborhood shop" feel. Loyal customers love to tell friends and family about how the business takes extra time to care. Taylor Stitch desires regular customers but they also want to *be* regulars in their neighborhood.

"Our customers send us thank-you and holiday cards," says Maher. "Sometimes they even send jams and other little gifts. It's amazing to receive such gifts from people that buy stuff from you. One of my favorite things to do is stop people on the street whom I see wearing our clothes and thank them."

Obviously taking the time to not just make the clothes by hand but *handcraft* the customer experience on a very human level pays off for Taylor Stitch. At a pop-up market a few years ago, Maher gave a pair of pants to a fellow vendor. That vendor now orders and sells pants for the store. "It's often the simple, human things that benefit everyone," advises Maher. "When you do good things with no expectations and don't force it, great things are bound to happen."

Question 10: How do you measure success?

Unlike some marketers, I love metrics and they don't scare me at all. I love seeing if something worked or did not. Branding is a little bit gut feel, a little bit art, a little bit timing, and a whole lot of intentional, focused activity. That activity can be measured over time through all the different tactics you employ.

Ultimately, we're all after the same metric: more sales. But not all marketing activities are meant to produce the same goals. You have to make your way to increased sales in small steps rather than a giant leap. People won't necessarily buy from you the first time they come in contact with you.

> You have to make your way to increased sales in small steps rather than a giant leap. People won't necessarily buy from you the first time they come in contact with you.

Different aspects of your marketing plan help to move prospects along towards that larger goal. A former manager of mine once termed this as "Taking prospects on a journey." But it all starts with that strong Brand Strategy and promise.

The steps to get to a sale are often called *the sales and marketing cycle.* Before customers buy from you, they need to pass through three other phases. For inexpensive, at-the-cash-register, impulse buys such as chewing gum, it may only take someone thirty seconds to go from the first to the last stage. But most other businesses need a bit longer lead time to get a prospect through these phases. Some high-tech software companies have complex cycles that take six to twelve months. The sales and marketing cycle defines the stages a prospective customer goes through when considering you:

- I am aware that you exist
- I educate myself and seek out more information about you and your product or service
- I consider you for my short-list and evaluate your product or service by imagining how I would personally benefit from it, conducting a trial or seeking out references
- I am ready to buy from you

As depicted in the figure below, marketers will often call these phases:

- Awareness
- Education
- Consideration or Evaluation
- Purchase

For each phase, put yourself in the prospective customer's shoes and visualize them interacting with you in various ways. Are they driving their car when the need for your product arises, or will they do extensive web research when buying such a thing? Do they first see your product at a trade show? What would they need when they leave your booth in order to move into the next phase? For each phase of the cycle, the customer has different information needs, so you must plan your marketing activities accordingly. Effective branding and messaging at each phase can also help move them along faster. What do they need to see and hear from you to move down the path? Different marketing activities correspond to each phase of the cycle, and branding has a role in all of them.

> Different marketing activities correspond to each phase of the cycle, and branding has a role in all of them.

As we discussed, brand informs all your marketing activities, but one of the most important roles brand can play is to get your prospects through the Awareness Phase. If your brand is so clear and concise it gets their attention, then you're on your way. The Brand provides the "air cover" necessary to make all your other marketing activities effective.

> The Brand provides the "air cover" necessary to make all your other marketing activities effective.

Once you establish the brand, you now have a relationship with the prospect that opens the door to promotions, direct marketing offers, and the like to lead them on a journey toward purchase. It's a numbers game: the more interest you can generate at the beginning of this funnel with a strong brand, the more sales you get out the other side. Just remember that brand must consistently carry through their entire experience or they will abandon the "journey."

When embarking on either a new business or rebranding an existing one, you can still assign metrics to see if you're gaining traction and actually moving people in the right direction. Once you design your new look and feel, implement your new messaging, build your revamped website, or clarify your offerings and benefits, what will you measure?

Let's take a closer look at how we can measure brand success.

Before someone can buy from you, they have to know you exist and interact with you. You can measure whether or not their interest is going up. You can look at both quantitative statistics, such as website visits, newsletter sign-ups, or in-store visitors.

Equally important is qualitative data, such as an increase in positive customer comments, more local buzz as a result of press mentions, or a general uptick in referral business.

Metrics don't have to be scary and they aren't always simply "number of products sold." Remember, it depends on what your brand or marketing plan includes and which phase the tactics you use are addressing. Metrics can be indicators of increased awareness that lead to eventual sales, such as the number of weekly website visitors or in-store shoppers per day. Eventually, it does all boil down to sales, but again, remember that different marketing tactics have different goals as you move a prospect down the path to the Purchase Phase. They can't just skip from A straight to Z. A press release, for example, could have a metric of "number of press hits achieved or articles mentioned," because you're trying to get the word out. That awareness may be a new prospect's first step on their journey to a sale with you, which you won't know until much later.

Soliciting and measuring feedback should be a constant activity, even if it's a simple question to a loyal customer, such as, "Joan, what do you think of our new store layout and signage?" This way you know if your branding and messaging are going in the right direction.

Have goals in mind before you embark on your brand efforts. This is key to any marketing activity, but especially important when working on your Brand Strategy. What are you trying to achieve? What are your goals? Why are you rebranding now?

Your goals may be as simple as getting twenty new customers a month or gaining three local newspaper press mentions this quarter. If you're rebranding to change perceptions or reposition your company, measure your success by doing a "before" survey, and then an "after" survey three months after you implement your new brand activities. Track and analyze social media chatter with built-in tools from Twitter, Facebook or third-parties such as Sprout Social, Social Mention, or Klout to gauge how people are talking about you.

EXERCISE:

Come up with five to ten metrics you will measure to ensure your Brand Strategy, and ultimately your marketing plan, is working effectively. Remember, these can be quantitative or qualitative. It's actually a good idea to use some of both, so you should record important anecdotal or general feedback you receive. Make your metrics realistic but time-based if you can, such as "twenty new newsletter sign-ups each month" or "fifty attendees to each monthly wine-tasting event." You can have one of the metrics be a sales number if you like, such as "generate $2 million in revenue this quarter," but keep that as your ultimate objective—the one to which all your branding and marketing activities, with their individual goals, will lead. Try to keep your brand goals more aligned to increasing visibility, awareness, or visits. For each customer, knowing about you and what you offer is the first step required for an eventual purchase.

Putting It All Together

At this point, you should have ten answers to all the questions above. You may need to go back and forth between some of these and revise your answers to earlier questions as you discover more about who you are and what you offer. For example, you may find your prices don't align with your ideal customer target, so you'll need to tweak this.

The Brand Strategy is a dynamic document that lives and breathes.

The Brand Strategy is a dynamic document that lives and breathes. It will refresh over time as you learn more about your customers, as your market changes, or as you adapt your offerings. While your core mission and values may stand the test of time, your brand expression, offerings, and differentiators will evolve over the life of your business. That's why you'll want to have solid answers to these brand questions—so you can start working smarter, not harder, and building a clear, consistent promise across all customer touchpoints. You want to ensure that you feel good about your benefits, your differentiators, your brand attributes, and your ideal customer before you go any further with marketing. Remember, the Brand Strategy will form the foundation for all your other marketing and even operational decisions, so it should be in a stable state.

If you completed these exercises, give yourself a pat on the back: you've come farther in creating a Brand Strategy than many other business owners, thus increasing your chances for success. Whether you've done the exercises in Word, PowerPoint, Excel, or even handwritten in a notebook, you'll want to use this information to influence all your business decisions. In Part 3 we'll discuss how to apply this Brand Strategy and bring it to life to achieve your goals.

Part 3:
Applying the Brand Strategy

NOW YOU HAVE A PRETTY LITTLE DOCUMENT with the answers to ten vital questions about your business. You've fleshed out your ideal customer and know him intimately. You focused on how you're different from each of your competitors. You expressed the reputation or image you want people to have of your company, through the brand attributes you selected.

Now what the heck do you do with it? This is where it all comes together, so hold onto your hat.

I have to be honest. Branding is a blend of art, science, and inspiration. Collecting data is important for our final conclusions, but most of the time, the magic happens during the questioning process itself, when clients talk through things. Images begin to emerge, patterns form, certain words come up over and over again. I can start to see when people authentically "light up" as they discuss their business or customers, versus when they're just paying lip service to something because they think they should. I take note of all of this during the process and probe further until we get to the core, whether we're talking about brand attributes, benefits, or fleshing out the ideal customer. In this way, you could say branding is part psychology as well. And that would make sense, given branding is all about persuasion, perception, and visceral emotion.

As much as I can, I'm going to show you how to use certain answers to snap together the important pieces. But I'd be lying if I said the process is purely academic. Research plays an important role in informing the brand elements, but pay attention to the process itself so you can see the real insights when they appear.

Remember our graphic from Part 1 showing Brand Strategy as the foundation for the rest of your marketing activities?

We saw it made practical sense to answer these ten questions before creating your Brand Building Blocks, as now you have an idea of what you want them to communicate to the world. We also saw how your Brand Strategy forms the basis of your marketing plan, and that Building Blocks can be mixed and matched to provide the content for the tactics you have chosen. Your Brand Building Blocks consist of:

- Company name
- Visual identity system: logo, colors, and style guide
- Key Messages Document: mission, vision, tagline, company descriptors, brand positioning statement, executive biographies, and a press release boilerplate

With these items in hand, you can mix and match them for any marketing plan you create. Your standard documentation can be used by your employees, contractors, designers, or writers to help them hit the ground running. This will help you communicate the brand consistently across all touchpoints and channels.

Brand Building Blocks: Choosing a Name

Now that you know who you are, what you offer, to whom you offer it, and what type of personality you want your organization to have, you're ready to choose a powerful name—whether for your company as a whole or a new product. Naming can be a tricky business, but there are some guidelines you can follow.

First, look at your business description from Question 1, and then consider the brand attributes. Knowing what you offer and how you want to be perceived can help you find the right tone for your name. If everything about your business screams formal and conservative, a name like Yahoo or Bing may not work for you.

Next, consider your ideal audience. To whom does the name need to appeal? A company appealing to seventy-year old retirees in a small midwestern town might need a different name than one appealing to twenty-five-year old graphic designers in Los Angeles. Your name should resonate for the audience, so perhaps you can use analogies or references that are age- or interest-appropriate to help them make sense of you.

Factor in your benefit statements and your greatest asset. Is there a name that conveys any of these? For example, if you're a spa and your benefits are serenity and relaxation, and your one greatest asset is that you have the most comfortable massage tables known to man, you may want to find a name that signifies comfort, rest, and tranquility. Another spa owner with a vivacious personality might emphasize how her services provide energy and vigor, so she picks a name evoking more spark and action. If certain names are overused, perhaps your brand lends itself to names or phrases in another language. Maybe our first spa could choose an Italian or French word that means comfort or serenity.

This is where the art comes in. People get paid a lot of money to come up with names, because it can be hard to pick just the right one. In addition, made-up names that actually work aren't that easy to create. Just look at the mess tech and Internet companies made with names that were just wacky and unpronounceable. I mean, really: Xoopit, Eskobo, Renkoo, Otavo, Oyogi, and Qoop? And before you lynch me, "Google" is actually derived from a real word, "googol," which means ten to the hundredth power, and it aligns with the company's original promise of finding any piece of information within the seemingly endless Internet labyrinth.

I have faith that by doing the Brand Strategy steps, your creative juices will flow and you'll find words or phrases that will resonate with you and your customers. You need to like the name yourself. After all, it's your business!

I've often come up with names while answering the ten questions. Certain words start bubbling to the surface. If you're stuck, get some close business partners or ideal customers together and run an informal focus group where you can brainstorm names. If you do this exercise with friends or family, I highly suggest getting business feedback on the names you come up with from ideal customers or business partners who may have a more objective point of view. What sounds great to your single, twenty-seven-year-old brother-in-law may tank with your ideal customer, a forty-five-year-old mother of two.

Be careful to choose just a few of the right people to get input from so you don't end up choosing a name by committee. You'll end up running in circles and never make a decision with too much input.

One of my favorite brainstorming tricks is using Thesaurus.com for inspiration. Type in the brand attributes or benefits you've chosen and see what pops up. You never know which words will hit just the right chord to inspire you.

Take a look at the competitors you listed in your Brand Strategy. Can you come up with a name that will stand out from that crowd? Do you see a theme emerging from their names that you can break away from? For example, many accountants, financial services companies, or jewelers carry a family name or the founder's name. This could be because trust and familiarity are the most important attributes for their target audience. If you want to stand out, however, consider picking a name that's more emotional or attribute-focused.

Marty Neumeier, author of *The Brand Gap* and *Zag* (New Riders Press) and an award-winning brand strategist, offers seven criteria for picking a good name:[13]

1. Distinctiveness: Does it stand out, especially from the competition? Does it separate well from ordinary text and speech, meaning does it avoid sounding too generic? He says the best brand names have the "presence" of a proper noun.

2. Brevity: Is it short enough to be easily recalled and used? Can it be shortened to a meaningless acronym or nickname? If so, avoid it.

3. Appropriateness: Is there a reasonable fit for the business purpose? If it would work just as well—or better—for another entity, keep looking.

4. Easy Spelling and Pronunciation: Will most people be able to spell the word after hearing it? Will they be able to pronounce it? As Marty states, a name shouldn't turn into a spelling test or make people feel stupid.

5. Likability: Will people enjoy using it? Is it intellectually stimulating or does it have a good "mouth feel"? Just ask how much I loved running around the house shouting, "Bing!" after Microsoft introduced their decision engine.

6. Extendability: Does the name have "legs?" Can it be visually interpreted or lend itself to a number of creative executions? Great names provide endless

opportunities for word play, Marty says. With my own firm, Red Slice, I have visual imagery of a red apple standing apart in a sea of green apples, and I carry over the fruit analogy with phrases like "take a bite," "fresh and juicy branding," and "crisp messaging." My newsletter is called "The Juice" and my signature branding offering is called The SLICE. There are endless ways I can play with this brand and the name and they all get back to my core attributes of fresh, smart, and sassy.

7. Protectability: Can it be trademarked? This is the science part of the equation. Can you get a good URL for your website that makes sense and won't confuse people? Some names are more defensible than others, making them safer and more valuable in the long run.

Marty says that high-imagery names are usually more memorable than low-imagery names. Many Greek or Latin root words are low imagery, because they don't help people form a mental picture (Accenture, Innoveda). But names like Apple or Betty Crocker create vivid mental images for people—and combine well with a visual treatment to create a memorable brand icon. One small business, Unicycle Creative, found exactly the right name that not only conveyed their business mission but also created opportunities for wordplay and brand extension, as you will see from their Brand at Work case study.

Brand at Work: Unicycle Creative

A name built upon a strong Brand Strategy can provide countless brand-extension ideas. Take Lorne Craig, president and owner of Unicycle Creative (Unicyclecreative.com), a Vancouver. BC-based marketing consultancy. The company's mission is to help sustainability-focused companies move forward with superior marketing strategy, branding, and communications. A sustainability-focused company may be producing a traditional product or service that uses fewer resources or creates less waste, giving them a product or service niche to improve ecological or social conditions.

Curious, sustainable, quirky, unique, and simple are the brand attributes Lorne wanted to communicate—and he found the perfect metaphor in "Unicycle Creative."

First of all, he showcased the fact that he's a one-person shop with partnerships and subcontractors. Second, the unicycle is quirky and attracts curiosity, much as the company name does—and Lorne himself sometimes rides one to meetings. Third, the unicycle metaphor provides opportunities for wordplay and brand analogies for his messaging.

"We ride economic cycles and business cycles while we recycle and ponder the carbon cycle," Lorne explains, "but there really is just one cycle. One ride. On a unicycle, there is no coasting. One is always in motion, always balancing, yet leaving only the smallest track upon the planet. Unicycle Creative is an efficient and streamlined agency, owned and operated by a single individual working with a network of partner businesses."

The brand influences Lorne's client selection and business practices. "We have turned down work in the past because the companies in question had not, in our opinion, done enough to improve their environmental or social impact," Lorne says. For an example of the types of clients that are aligned with Unicycle's brand, he worked with Canadian retailer London Drugs to share how they are quietly improving their environmental footprint. Unicycle Creative named the campaign "What's the Green Deal?" This name is deliberately phrased as a question, because it's all about the company and its customers working together to find sustainability answers. Just like with Unicycle's name, this campaign name stems from a clear brand strategy and extends across product features, recycling programs, and corporate initiatives. Most importantly, it is nonjudgmental. "Every person and company is in their own place on their sustainable journey. They can define 'green' for themselves and move forward," Lorne says. The program has been running since 2008 and has been recognized locally and nationally for its results.

He also tries to partner and support other sustainable businesses in his work: printers who use eco-friendly inks or suppliers who use recycled materials. His own business cards were created from items found in his recycle bin, garnering him national recognition from Applied Arts Magazine. Lorne relies heavily on his blog (Greenbriefs.ca) as his main marketing vehicle, allowing him to comment on green marketing issues, generate feedback, and approach new clients without sending a single sheet of paper.

Brand Building Blocks: Creating Your Visual Identity System

Now that you have your Brand Strategy all thought out and you know who you're trying to reach with what messages, you're ready to design a logo, packaging, and other visual identity pieces. Even though nine times out ten, businesses start with the logo and work backwards, if you're a new business, I implore you to do things in the right order. The clients I talk to who didn't work this way often wasted money and time on designers who just didn't get it. One client went through four different designers and thousands of dollars trying to get her logo just right. It might not be the designer's fault: as we saw earlier, a designer's job is to take a message and communicate it visually. If he receives no guidance on the true message, or who it needs to attract in what way, then he is grasping at straws.

Don't underestimate the power of a logo or any visual design. Hopefully you'll be living with this visual identity for a while and will spend money on marketing, production, and customer service to make it *mean something* to your audience. Aren't you asking a logo to do part of the heavy lifting for you and communicate something before you even say a word?

Don't underestimate the power of a logo or any visual design.

I know, I know. A logo is just a graphic, a picture. How can you communicate everything about a business and what you provide in one little thing? The truth is, you can't communicate *everything*, but you can communicate *something*. You can communicate what the experience "under the wrapper" will be like for them and establish expectations.

Even though taste is subjective, aesthetics do matter subconsciously to human perceptions. I once asked a creative director, "But what difference does it really make? If the client wants to tweak something this way or that, shouldn't we be okay with that?"

He sighed and said, "Yes, Maria, but there are fundamental truths to good design, balance, placement, and typography that the human eye will absorb and base opinions on. And the client can't fight that. It's our job to create a logo or ad that stays true to human design principles as a whole and carefully balances that with personal preferences—otherwise what are they paying us for?"

This is true of logos, colors, shapes, typefaces, placement, and size—all of these make an impression and mean something to a customer. While it's true that a logo I think is cheesy might seem elegant to someone else, a great designer knows where universal human truths come into play. Many business owners create logos on the cheap, resulting in poor color choices, even worse font choices, and placement that's either too busy and jarring, or sparse and unbalanced. After all the logos I've seen and studied, I can spot the poor-spacing decisions, logos that give me a headache because there's no focal point, or the ones that won't translate well to other media. And I'm not even a skilled designer.

When designing your logo, you want to factor in your business description, benefits, brand attributes, and ideal customer. You can use colors to convey mood and status. Are you a retro company and want to evoke themes from the past? Then you might pick colors from the '70s or '80s. Are you soft and serene? Then pastel or lighter hues may win out over bright, garish shades.

One visual identity mistake some companies make is to assume that since they're marketing to women, they need to incorporate pink. Depending on the type of woman (remember your detailed ideal customer profile), she may be sick of that color or think you're pandering to her. Urban working women may be attracted to a broad range of modern colors you'd find in magazines like *Dwell*.

We learned from Bridget Perez of TRAY Creative (TRAYcreative.com) in Part 1 how color influences the buying decision. Her design work involves finding the right logo and color palette to communicate what you do and why you are different. Bridget says color can evoke strong emotional responses and trigger memories for people. Colors also have specific meaning. For example, green signifies *go*, *money*, or *nature*, while red signifies *stop*, *heat*, or *love*. Some meanings are universal, while others are cultural. Sometimes gender also plays a role in color perception.

> When it comes to color, the bottom line is to be mindful of why you're selecting it and what it will communicate. Don't just pick your favorite colors.

When it comes to color, the bottom line is to be mindful of why you're selecting it and what it will communicate. Don't just pick your favorite colors. Think about your audience—the people with whom you're trying to connect. What colors will resonate with them and evoke the appropriate emotional responses about your business? Also consider the industry you're in and who you want to be within the industry. What colors do your competitors use? Is it more strategic to blend in with them, or stand out? In what way can color make your business distinctive? Will the colors you choose translate consistently across different media? Are they too trendy and will they become dated? Do they unintentionally evoke negative connotations? With a little research on the meaning of color, your customers, and your competitors, you'll be able to make a well-informed decision about the colors for your company.

The second important factor is font, or typeface. I see many businesses who say they want to be elegant, high-end, and refined, but the company name on their logo is written in a clunky and heavy font—nothing refined or elegant about it. Others want to appeal to a modern sensibility, but they use a traditional, old-fashioned serif font.

Ayesha Mathews-Wadhwa, "chief pixel bender" for PixInk Design (Pixinkdesign.com), says that font adds the sparkle to a logo or company identity. "It's crucial for brands to pick a font not simply for its popularity, but for the right message it communicates about the brand," she says. "This enhances the features of the brand visually."

Is your brand timeless, vintage, and classic? A script or serif font (the fonts with little "tags" on the ends of each letter, such as you see in Times New Roman) may be appropriate. Serif fonts have been around for centuries and denote dependability.

Ayesha says you also need to consider where this font will be seen. While some fonts may work for a logo, you might want to be careful using certain fonts for your website copy. "The serifs could clutter a paragraph on the web, but shouldn't be avoided in logos or other main design elements," Ayesha cautions.

Sans serifs are used for a modern, clean, sleek look. They reek of efficiency, simplicity, and innovation. The opposite of serif fonts, these look great on a small screen.

Think about your brand attributes when picking the font for both your logo and your copy. Is your company loud, energetic, fun, and imaginative? Maybe you should consider a decorative font. These are great for brands geared towards entertainment and children. Is your brand strong, confident, and manly? Pick fonts with square, right angles. Bold and other heavily structured fonts clearly communicate this message. A transportation company, financial institution, durable-products distributor, or law office might consider these. Is the brand feminine, graceful, beautiful, and delicate? Script fonts are a good solution.

"Fonts carry the most important first impressions to the customer in the form of collateral, letterhead, web pages, promotional items, advertisements, business cards, brochures, and package designs," says Ayesha. "They can stimulate opinions about company character, moral aptitude, and credibility. It is vital to get the right help for this responsibility."

Visual identity is an important clue to what your organization is all about and what people can expect. As we see in the Brand at Work case study which follows, TCHO Chocolate put a lot of effort into creating a breakout visual identity that conveys quality and differentiation—clues to the experience awaiting the lucky customer "under the wrapper."

Brand at Work: TCHO Chocolate

When it comes to crafting innovative chocolate unlike anything else out there, TCHO (*pronounced "choh" with a silent T*) is obsessed—and proud of it. This San Francisco-based craft chocolate manufacturer is obsessed with creating amazing chocolate from "bean to bar."

Founder Timothy Childs learned about cacao while traveling in South America. A classic San Francisco technology entrepreneur, he became obsessed with the art of craft chocolate making and asked why there was nothing like this in the U.S. Upon his return, he teamed up with a chocolate making expert, rented space and played around with ways to make a fantastic product. He soon thereafter teamed up with Louis Rossetto who went on to become TCHO's CEO for five years and was responsible for leading the company's positioning, branding and avant-garde packaging achievements.

TCHO's brand is clearly rooted as "Silicon Valley start-up meets San Francisco food culture." This means marrying quality products, ongoing innovation and social responsibility, all of which are hallmarks of their hometown region. TCHO's key to living out these three core brand values begins at the source.

"Our greatest differentiation is that we literally work from the ground up to source the best cacao, which is the foundation of everything we do. We don't just *buy* good beans, we *help make* the best beans so we can craft genuine chocolate the way it was meant to be made, without having to fake it or add things" says John Kehoe, vice president of sourcing. This mission led to TCHOSource, an innovative sourcing program that goes beyond Fair Trade to partner directly with grower co-ops in South America and Africa. TCHOSource works with farmers and cooperatives to help them grow and produce the highest quality cacao: from varietal selection to fermentation and drying. "We empower growers to create more than just a commodity product, but to become true flavor-bean producers," says John, who is on the ground with growers several times each year.

TCHO's ideal customers, described as "foodies and professionals," value such quality and are eager to learn about the process. The company believes in making customers as knowledgeable as possible and offers a cacao mini-education, factory tours and tastings—all for free. Doing so enhances not just enjoyment of the product but an appreciation for TCHO's mission and quality commitment. "We realize this isn't the way chocolate is normally done, but we don't believe in 'normal:' TCHO sets a higher standard," says Brad Kintzer, head chocolate maker. Like a fine wine maker, he's involved in determining the right mix of Ecuadorian, Peruvian, or Ghanian chocolate that go into each bar to create unique flavor experiences.

As for living out their value of innovation, TCHO created a custom iPhone/iPad app to control and monitor the primary equipment in its pre-production lab, as well as remotely view the production facility through a digital camera system. They also created a Flavor Wheel to tune each of their chocolates. Akin to the qualities discussed in the wine industry, the Flavor Wheel serves not only to help TCHO search the world for just the right beans, but also helps their customers discover flavor nuances in a fresh new way.

The product is so different that the company must position it differently. Anything but a mass market brand, it is endorsed by high-end chefs and restaurants. Distributed in specialty food stores around the U.S., the product comes at a higher price point and its unique and modern visual identity stands out on the shelf, inviting customers to try it. "Our price point and unique fine-design packaging makes new customers curious," says Brad. "But that's the easy part. At the end of the day, if the product doesn't live up to the brand promise of the higher price and cool packaging, why bother? Our brand is really about what's on the inside. What is your *experience* when eating this chocolate? Your price and packaging tells a story but the product has to live up to it. That's how you become a respected authority."

That's a delicious brand obsession, by any measure.

Brand Building Blocks: Crafting Your Key Messages

Now that you have your Brand Strategy baked, you're ready to build your key corporate messages. You can put these together into a Key Messages Document and refer to it over and over again. Not only will this save time when you're asked for information, but you'll maintain consistency in all places where people see you and your brand. In addition, you get the added benefit of having a cheat sheet for employees to ensure their messages are consistent and clear. The last thing you want is people making up their own versions of your company description or tagline on the fly.

The Key Messages Document I use with my clients includes the following:

- Brand positioning statement
- Mission
- Vision
- Tagline
- 25-, 50-, and 100-word company descriptors
- Benefits
- Differentiators
- Executive bios
- Press release boilerplate
- Elevator pitch

Brand Positioning Statement

The brand positioning statement is a paragraph that encapsulates the entire Brand Strategy process and all your answers. Most of the time, you'll be able to send all ten of these questions and answers to a designer or writer as background info. But sometimes, you want to sum it all up in an explanatory paragraph for your designer or writer—or even for yourself.

You may also include it in orientation materials to ensure your employees understand what you're all about. This is where you can use those analogies to other brands, characters, and famous people you thought through in your brand attributes answer.

This statement is for internal or agency use only—it's not meant to be customer-facing. Later on, you'll develop customer-ready copy that is informed by this statement. For now, it's just a way of articulating for yourself what you want your business to be and how you'd like it to be perceived.

Here's a brand-positioning statement example from a massage and bodywork client:

> "Alinga Bodywork is the Anthropologie of the bodywork field, offering a unique, creative, individual approach to bodywork (massage, Reiki, and BodyTalk) combined with attentive and personalized service that is in tune with the way you express yourself and your personal truth. It provides busy women with high value yet affordable services that go beyond just surface pampering to something deeper and more lasting. Unlike pure massage therapists, Andrea uses the body as an access point to specifically identify what is holding you back by releasing physical tension and unprocessed emotions. This release helps you get unstuck creatively and emotionally. Sessions at Alinga provide a lasting investment in your self-development that goes beyond pure pampering.
>
> Alinga is focused on balance, action, forward movement, and progress. It propels clients to the next level by shifting them out of stagnation and into action in their lives or work by using a body-centered approach to process the physical and emotional/energetic issues holding them back. It opens them up

to new possibilities, giving them the clarity and the confidence to manifest a new reality, whether that be launching or expanding a business; jumping feet first into exploring art, music, or higher education; or creating space in daily life to be more present in the moment and connected to the body."

This brand-positioning statement was a carefully worded summary of the ten answers. The business owner created this summary after putting time and thought into her audience, brand attributes, differentiators, and customer benefits. She incorporated analogies to better-known brands to bring certain images and feelings to mind. We know which slot she wants to occupy in someone's brain. Certain words and phrases came up over and over during the process and we paid attention to those when we built her brand positioning, as well as her tagline and mission statement.

Mission and Vision

The mission and vision also become clear as you move through the ten-question Brand Strategy process. As you think about your company's reason for being, your goals, the image you want to project, and the people you serve, you begin expanding your definition of what you want your company to be. I find just talking to a business owner and asking, "Why did you start this business?" can yield the seeds of a mission or vision statement. They use certain words or phrases over and over again. As you think through your Brand Strategy, certain themes that consistently emerge will be strong clues to your mission and vision. The mission and vision not only help you keep the end in mind at all times, they will also inspire your customers—and your employees.

> The mission and vision not only help you keep the end in mind at all times, they will also inspire your customers—and your employees.

Yes, I know your primary goal is to make (or raise) money, but customers, donors and employees want to connect with your organization on a deeper level. They want to know their buying choices and work efforts are relevant to a higher goal. This motivates people to form loyal connections.

Mike Michalowicz, the irrepressible marketing consultant and author of *The Pumpkin Plan* and *The Toilet Paper Entrepreneur,* advises small organizations to ensure that their purpose transcends time and money. "The primary goal of your business is not to make tons of money," he says. "You're here to authentically express yourself through your work, and money is a vehicle for this. People try to build messages that make the most money but that's a mistake. Start with your purpose and build a brand that presents your most authentic values and beliefs. This is what will bring you the most money. It's an upward spiral."

Mission

Your mission statement is a precise definition of what your organization does on a daily basis and what you want to accomplish. It should describe the business you're in and provide a definition of why the organization exists. Try and keep this to one or two sentences in length. Some example mission statements:

- "Make flying good again." (Virgin America)
- "Our mission: to inspire and nurture the human spirit—one person, one cup, and one neighborhood at a time." (Starbucks)
- "The mission of Southwest Airlines is dedication to the highest quality of Customer Service delivered with a sense of warmth, friendliness, individual pride, and Company Spirit." (Southwest Airlines)
- "To provide effective means for the prevention of cruelty to animals throughout the United States." (ASPCA)

- "Women for Women International provides women survivors of war, civil strife, and other conflicts with the tools and resources to move from crisis and poverty to stability and self-sufficiency, thereby promoting viable civil societies. We're changing the world one woman at a time." (Women for Women International)

My personal bias is that such mission statements as "To provide the best customer service and product quality" are too generic. Try to put your mission statement in the context of what you do, while still leaving room to expand your offerings. The mission at Red Slice, my firm, is "To engage, inform, and delight." This has to do with providing marketing and branding strategies that get attention (engage), let audiences know a bit more about the organization and why they're different (inform), and provide a connection (delight). Incidentally, this is my personal mission in all my writing, speaking, and workshop pursuits as well, so it applies broadly to other services while leaving room for growth.

Small businesses can create a mission statement so inspiring they may not require a vision statement. But if you have a loftier goal in mind for the organization's future, then a vision statement is a great way to frame that.

Vision

Rebecca Rodskog of Rodskog Change Consulting (Rodskog. com) helps businesses and individuals transform for better results. As an experienced change management consultant and personal development professional, Rebecca is often tasked with crafting vision and mission statements for complex projects so that organizations don't lose sight of the end goal. She also creates mission and vision statements for individuals. Rebecca advises clients who are creating a vision statement to ask themselves: "What is our ideal preferred future?" and be sure the answer...

- Draws on the beliefs, mission, and environment of the organization
- Describes what you want to see in the future
- Is positive and inspiring
- Doesn't assume the system will have the same framework as it does today
- Is open to dramatic modifications to current organization, methodology, teaching techniques, facilities, etc.

Next, ask yourself:
- Where will my company be in the long term?
- Will it be the premier provider of a particular product or service? Will it be in the top ten international players in a particular market?
- What is the ultimate "to be" state for my company?

You may not require an actual, written vision statement, as long as you can paint a clear, compelling picture that drives the business forward. These could be ideals or lofty goals that rally the internal troops and help customers connect with you. Below you'll find sample vision statements from several companies. You'll note these contain ambitious visions that go beyond day-to-day operations and the specific market spaces in which these organizations play today. They paint a picture of an ideal future if the organization does well:

Women for Women International envisions a world where no one is abused, poor, illiterate, or marginalized; where members of communities have full and equal participation in the processes that ensure their health, well-being and economic independence, and where everyone has the freedom to define the scope of their life, their future, and strive to achieve their full potential. (Women for Women International)

I believe that this nation should commit itself to achieving the goal, before this decade is out, of landing a man on the moon and returning him safely to the earth. (President John F. Kennedy, 1961)

Coca Cola's vision statement is actually a multipart credo:

People: Be a great place to work where people are inspired to be the best they can be.

Portfolio: Bring to the world a portfolio of quality beverage brands that anticipate and satisfy people's desires and needs.

Partners: Nurture a winning network of customers and suppliers; together, we create mutual, enduring value.

Planet: Be a responsible citizen that makes a difference by helping build and support sustainable communities.

Profit: Maximize long-term return to shareowners while being mindful of our overall responsibilities.

Productivity: Be a highly effective, lean, and fast-moving organization.

In summary, your mission is what drives you on a day-to-day basis. It's the reason your product or service is in existence, and it defines the *why* behind the thing you're creating.

Your vision is the end state: what you ultimately want your company to become and the impact you want to have on your customers and the world. Your mission and vision create the framework and inspiration your organization and its employees need to be successful. An old Japanese proverb eloquently states the important symbiotic relationship between vision and action: *Vision without action is a daydream. Action without vision is a nightmare.*

Tagline

The tagline is another element that almost always falls out of the Brand Strategy process. It's a short, punchy, memorable phrase that can be used in advertising and on company materials. The tagline sums up what you're all about in a memorable way, either in actual words or the tone of those words. A tagline could accompany your logo at all times, and in fact be part of it. Or you can have a tagline you only use on certain materials, not officially integrated with your logo. The choice is yours.

As you talk through your vision, goals, and benefits, certain words and sayings will appear again and again. Jot down the little inspirations that pop up during the process, even if they don't apply to the question you're answering. This is exactly how I've stumbled upon great taglines for my clients.

> You want a tagline to be short and sweet, not a long, descriptive sentence. You want something people will remember.

You want a tagline to be short and sweet, not a long, descriptive sentence. You want something people will remember. Alliterations often work well, or several short words or phrases. Here are some examples:

- *"Pampering with Purpose"* (for a massage and bodywork business)

- *"Informed Girls. Empowered Women"* (for a company providing advice for parents of young girls who are going through puberty)

- *"Branch Out. Live Richly!"* (for a career consultant who helps people with multiple passions define financially and emotionally rewarding careers that encompass them all)

- *"Grow"* (for a consultant and life coach who helps individuals and organizations deal with and adapt to change in an opportunistic way)

- *"Straight Talk Meets Straight Tech"* (for an IT consulting firm that detests jargon and focuses on results)

You want to avoid a boring, descriptive sentence as a tagline, such as, "Helping women build and create their own businesses." While that may indeed be the organization's mission, it isn't memorable (or short) enough to use in advertising or with a logo. Instead, take inspiration from Giggle (Giggle.com), a specialty baby brand featuring products, content, eCommerce, retail stores, mobile-enabled registry and other resources for new parents. This is what the company *does*. But their actual brand tagline is catchier and more fun: "*Happy. Healthy. Baby.*"

Here are other examples of memorable taglines:

- "The ultimate driving machine"
- "Just do it"
- "Made from the best stuff on Earth"
- "You're in good hands"
- "Fly the friendly skies"
- "Does a body good"

One last thing to note is the difference between taglines and campaign slogans. *Taglines* are all-encompassing and represent the company at a macro level. They last for awhile, until perhaps the company rebrands. A *slogan* is a theme used in a specific multi-channel ad campaign, and when the campaign ends, the campaign "tagline" (slogan) goes away. Examples of this would be Southwest Airlines' "Grab your bags. It's on" recent ad campaign; Bud Light's "The difference is drinkability"; or Coca Cola's "Open Happiness." These are not corporate taglines per se, but specific campaign slogans that are temporal in nature. If you have a limited budget and time, it might be best to find one permanent tagline to hang your hat on and get in front of customers for a longer period of time, rather than confuse them with different slogans.

Company Descriptors

Standard company descriptors will be a useful tool for your business. Inevitably, you'll need to provide someone with a short description of your firm: for a trade show program, an ad link on a partner site, or when you sponsor a direct mail piece. You're often bound by space and character constraints, so it's helpful to prepare 25-word, 50-word, and 100-word descriptors in advance. This also helps when others within the organization need to send a description out as part of a proposal or brochure.

Many folks use this verbiage on the "About" page of their website. Again, you should create this in advance, because you don't want everyone coming up with their own definitions and inventing messages on the fly.

To create this information, use elements of the company description you created in Question 1, combined with a few benefits you provide and something about the audience you serve. You also may want to list your website address in the description, so people can go there for more information. Here's an example from a past client:

> CareerBranches is the premier boutique career-design agency for multi-talented individuals who simply can't pick just one career. CareerBranches's coaching and career-design services help modern-day "Renaissance Personalities" claim their place in today's specialist society and thrive in their careers and lives. Explore the possibilities at Careerbranches.com.

The description takes into account what she does (coaching and career-design services), for whom she does it (people who have multiple talents and have trouble choosing just one career path), and gives her URL for more information. If she ever sponsors an event or has a partner link next to her logo on another site, she can use this same description everywhere to ensure consistency and clarity.

Here's another example, from an eCommerce client:

> **"** Dot Girl Products offers products and resources that help parents comfortably talk to and reassure their young daughters about womanhood. Our signature product, The Dot Girls First Period Kit, is a stylish and discreet carrying case with all the essentials a girl needs for her first period, including pads, calendar, scented wipes, heating pad, and a Guide to Menstruation. The Guide answers all of the questions a young girl may have and helps parents easily and lovingly start the conversation. Our vision is to create empowered, informed, and happy young women who take a positive first step into womanhood. **"**

This descriptor incorporated the vision of helping create healthy, empowered young women as a result of their work. It also describes the product they sell and who they serve (parents of young girls). With this standard company descriptor at the ready, the company is secure in the fact that any employee or partner can provide a consistent descriptor for materials or sponsorship.

> With a standard company descriptor at the ready, the company is secure in the fact that any employee or partner can provide a consistent descriptor for materials or sponsorship.

When working as a marketing director for companies in the past, I was always ready when a trade show organizer asked for a one-line descriptor for the conference guide or when a partner asked for a few lines to accompany our logo on their website. I recommend you start by building the longest one (100 words or less) first, so you can include everything you want, and then editing down to the most crucial points, rather than starting with the shortest one and building up.

Benefits and Differentiators

Your Key Messages Document should list the main corporate benefits and core differentiators you want to tout in all of your messaging. You came up with this list in the Brand Strategy process, and placing it in the Key Messages Document captures everything in one place for easy reference. Some small businesses can get away with a simple bulleted list of benefits and differentiators, but others, especially technology companies, expand on this concept and create a *messaging platform*. This matrix is used as an outline for all other written communications—sales presentations, website copy, brochures, etc. It contains:

- The company's overall, high-level value proposition
- Three main benefits the company offers
- Three main capabilities that support each benefit claim (How do you provide that benefit?)
- Three main proof points or features that support each capability (What proof do you have that you can do what you say you can do? Why are you able to offer that capability?)

Some businesses do this process in reverse, especially product or technology companies. They first look at all their product features and group them under certain functions or capabilities. Then they group and roll up those capabilities under certain benefit headings. For example, you could look at features of a car: accident early-warning system, side-impact airbags, and ergonomic safety belts. With these features, the carmaker can state that it provides state-of-the-art automotive safety technology. That capability in turn offers the end benefit to customers of "keeping your family safe."

Listing your benefits and differentiators will ensure your employees as well as hired writers and designers are clear on what your business offers to customers and what you feel is most important. Your advertising copy will consistently reflect the right points. When customers who see your messages in multiple places and on multiple occasions see and hear the same thing, the message is more likely to stick in their minds. Also, your messaging platform can later be condensed to craft the Elevator Pitch, which we'll talk about in a moment.

A bulleted list of your differentiators can quickly bring someone up to speed on the main ways you're better than your competition. Rather than let a writer, an employee, or even a partner invent their own interpretation, you create a master list from which everyone works to ensure all communications consistently emphasize the right points.

Executive Biographies

The executive biography, or bio, is exactly that: a short, one-paragraph biography for each key executive that you can use on the website or for introductions at speaking engagements. I include biographies in the Key Messages Document because you may want to emphasize certain experiences in the executive's background that will back up your Brand Strategy. Many organizations ignore this as a communication vehicle and whip up a boilerplate bio rather than use it as another simple yet effective branding opportunity.

> Many organizations ignore executive biographies as a communication vehicle and whip up a boilerplate bio rather than use it as another simple yet effective branding opportunity.

All of your corporate messaging pieces should work together to support the brand, and bios are no exception. For example, if your brand is playful and casual, you won't write a stiff, boring bio for your website. You may want to talk about favorite trips the executives have taken or activities they enjoy.

If your brand is devoted to community philanthropy, you'll want to highlight the volunteer organizations to which the key executives donate their time and talents. Should your brand emphasize family, home, and work-life balance, you'll mention the hobbies or family interests of each executive. If you sell athletic apparel and accessories, maybe you want to mention each executive's favorite sport. The point is that a bio is yet another vital customer touchpoint to help solidify your organization's image and verbally communicate your brand promise.

You can use your bio to jazz things up and differentiate yourself. Starting your bio with what you're passionate about or your personal mission can be far more interesting and engaging than bland résumé regurgitation. Every communication with your audience can help build the brand in your audience's mind, and a bio is no exception.

Press Boilerplate

Your press release boilerplate is the final standardized tool you'll need in your messaging bag of tricks. As you write press releases to promote your business, you need to include standard boilerplate language at the end of each one. You often see these in the form of "About" sections at the end of the release. This gives the media background on your company, so you don't have to spend a paragraph talking about it in the release itself and can jump right to the meat of the news story. The press release boilerplate is derived from the company descriptor, with a few other facts thrown in, such as the year you were founded, where people can find your products or services, and awards you may have won. The boilerplate often lists a general sales contact phone number or website address. Here's an example from a 2013 press release[14] for Seattle, Washington's Theo Chocolate:

❝ Since 2006, Theo Chocolate has been committed to responsibly sourcing and manufacturing the highest quality chocolate in the world. As the first bean-to-bar maker of Organic, Fair Trade, Fair for Life, and Non-GMO certified chocolate in North America, Theo is creating delicious products while working to improve livelihoods and protect the environment in farm and factory communities alike. To find Theo chocolate at a retailer near you and learn more about how the company puts its passion into practice, visit theochocolate.com. **❞**

Crafting a Killer Elevator Pitch

I'm often amazed at how many clients come to me for help on the elevator pitch before they've done due diligence on their Brand Strategy. You'll have difficulty knowing what needs to be communicated in an elevator pitch if you don't yet have a good sense of your benefits, differentiators, and ideal customers.

Many a Silicon Valley start-up was funded via a catchy elevator pitch. But this simple marketing tool does more than help you get investors. You'll use this handy tool anytime you speak in public about your business. I've seen many small business owners stumble when introducing themselves at a networking event or panel discussion because they have not prepared a crisp and clear elevator pitch . Sometimes they even leave the audience wondering if they provide a product or a service, the most fundamental point about what they do.

An elevator pitch is so named because if you were on an elevator with someone who asked about your organization, you'd only have so many floors to give a clear answer. This pitch is your thirty-second to one-minute long response to the question, "What does your company do?"

An elevator pitch is your thirty-second to one-minute response to the question, "What does your company do?"

The pitch requires you to go one step deeper on your claims, citing examples and proof points of how or why you do this. It's the story you tell to intrigue listeners, giving them a desire to learn more about your firm and what you do. One framework for creating your elevator pitch is to combine the answers about your company description, your benefits, and your differentiators into one short, smooth, and flowing story.

Start with an overall proposition sentence—best to make this mission-driven. For example, "*Yoga Yoga offers yoga and meditation classes that help clients connect to their center and balance their lives.*"

Cite three main benefits you offer. If you have a list of ten, then pick the three most important things you want people to remember. The more information you throw at people, the less anything will stick, so carefully choose only three main points. The idea is to pique their interest, not tell them everything in thirty seconds. Here are Yoga Yoga's three main benefits: "*We increase energy, reduce stress, and improve your body's flexibility.*"

Cite a capability that illustrates how you deliver each benefit. This is the "And what I mean by that is...." description of your benefit point. For example, for "reduce stress" our owner might say: "*Our yoga classes give you a quiet space to meditate and breathe, and the practice can help you take a break from your hectic life.*"

Cite a proof point for each capability—tell me why only you can make this claim. "*Our clients report healthy or lowered blood pressures as a result of working with us.*"

End with a one-sentence summary. This could even be your tagline. "*Yoga Yoga connects your body and mind so you can live in great harmony.*"

You may not have time to say all of this in every instance, but you can scale the model to fit the allotted time. For example, if you only have fifteen seconds, give your opening line, three main benefits, and your closing summary.

An elevator pitch is meant to be spoken, so use words you are comfortable actually saying and yet still convey passion and excitement. It is vital to have something prepared for you, your partners and your employees to use when networking, public speaking, and just generally telling others about the business.

> An elevator pitch is meant to be spoken, so use words you are comfortable actually saying and yet still convey passion and excitement.

The closing line is especially important to nail down, because you don't want to commit the biggest networking sin: ending your pitch with, "Okay, so, um, yeah, that's it. That's what we do." As a track coach of mine once said, "You need to finish strong!" You want to leave a confident impression in people's minds, which is why I suggest ending with a tagline. Since your employees represent you, make sure they know the pitch as well. They can make the words their own over time, so they don't all sound like robots, but you can rest assured that no matter which employee a customer meets, they'll get a consistent business description.

At many software companies for which I worked, we gathered feedback from employees before crafting the pitch, to see how they described the business and what resonated for them. This gave us their buy-in. Then we asked every salesperson to memorize it and even quizzed them on it at sales meetings.

Keeping your Messages Clear and Simple

When you express your Brand Strategy in words and develop these key messages, please don't forget what communication specialist Alexandra Franzen talked about in Part 1: keep things simple.

An exercise I play with clients is to ask them to tell me how they would describe their organization to their grandmother or their five-year-old daughter. Often, what they say is exactly what they need to communicate to adults. "Albert Einstein once said that if you can't explain it to a six-year-old, you don't understand it yourself!" Alexandra says. "If it takes you eighty-five paragraphs to explain something, you're probably not clear on it. Particularly in the online space, people have a shorter attention span. Customers will be skimming your site, flipping around, spending just a few seconds here and there. You need to be exceptionally simple."

Alexandra advises taking lessons from scientist, astronomer, and author Carl Sagan, or beloved children's TV show host Mister Rogers, or English broadcaster and naturalist David Attenborough. "These people were legendary educators who had mass appeal because of their incredible skill in distilling information so that anyone from any background could understand. This is what makes them so beloved and great. Distillation is not the same as *dumbing down*. It's about expressing the purest essence of an idea—without any unnecessary clutter."

When crafting your messages, ditch the jargon where you can. Of course, you need to speak the language of your industry but don't overcomplicate things. The goal is to make your target audience feel competent, not to make them feel dumb. "When crafting copy for your business," says Alexandra, "above all, your job is to make the person reading feel *competent*. If they think to themselves, 'I don't understand the words on the screen in front of me, and now I feel dumb,' they'll probably click away from your website and never come back. But if they think to themselves, 'I get this, and it sounds like precisely what I need!' they'll be excited to take the next step."

Determining Your Marketing Investments

Now that you have a Brand Strategy mapped out and you've crafted a visual identity and messaging, you're prepared to make smart investment decisions. Remember when we created the ideal-customer profile in rich detail? Now you can decide which marketing vehicles will get you in front of the right customers—and which ones will be a total waste of time.

Review your ideal-customer profile and that person's "day in the life." Are they watching TV or do they mostly get information from the web? Do they listen to the radio or read magazines? What organizations and clubs do they belong to? As you review this information, you'll start to see interesting marketing opportunities to guide your decisions.

This is where you decide if social media is the right tactic for you—and if so, which social media channels to use. Many platforms enable you to microtarget your message based on your specific target audience. For example, businesses that target Internet-savvy brides-to-be might be interested to know that in 2013, the top life event posted by Facebook users was "Added a Relationship/Got Engaged/Got Married."[15] Armed with that information, you can then use profile demographics and keywords to reach even more specific users, such as eco-brides, fashion-conscious brides, athletic brides, etc.

Until you know your own audience intimately, any demographic or behavioral data will be useless because you won't know if that's who you want to reach. When placing an ad or sponsoring an event, you need to research or ask for an audience profile or demographic data. Even better, do they have psychographic data profiling the wants, needs, and behaviors of the audience? Then you can decide if that vehicle fits your ideal customer. Don't be lulled by promises of quantity when it's quality you're after. For example, suppose a large conference attracts five thousand moms and asks your mom-focused business to sponsor a booth. But what if those moms are in a lower-income bracket and have no disposable income to spend on your high-end luxury product? Or your product is for toddler moms, but the show only attracts moms of college students? This is an extreme example, but nine times out of ten, small business owners *assume* something will be a good marketing opportunity based on quantity, and they don't ask the right questions to dig deeper. They also don't factor in whether the brand of the event, magazine, or website is a good fit with their own brand. This is because they haven't defined their own brand clearly enough.

Now that you have a Brand Strategy, you can better decide which places align well with your brand and which could damage it. For example, a high-end luxury jeweler may not choose to spend their limited marketing budget on *The National Enquirer* or sponsoring a pay-per-view wrestling match, no matter how great the advertising deal sounds. They want to advertise and partner with vehicles that hit the same ideal customer and have a similar brand caliber that won't damage brand equity. Choosing the right marketing vehicles is one of the most important ways to ensure your brand is consistently represented.

> Choosing the right marketing vehicles is one of the most important ways to ensure your brand is consistently represented.

The Brand at Work case study on CRAVE that follows shows how a well-crafted ideal-customer profile and Brand Strategy can focus your efforts and avoid costly tactics that are not a good fit for your business.

Brand at Work: CRAVE

Serial entrepreneur Melody Biringer has a firm vision of her ideal customer, and that has made all the difference to the success of The CRAVE Company (TheCraveCompany.com). CRAVE is an innovative women's media company that connects urban gals in over thirty cities worldwide to the sassiest, gutsiest, most inspiring people they need to know in town through parties, gatherings, and online networking. What initially started in 2001 as a way for Melody to spend more time relaxing, indulging, shopping, and styling with her girlfriends has turned into a multicity international venture. The secret is that the CRAVE brand has local presence in many of its markets, such as CRAVEseattle and CRAVEamsterdam, so it creates personal local connections.

Melody targets two distinct audiences: female consumers and female business owners. On one side, her parties and events attract the urban-minded woman in her thirties or forties who's an independent thinker and fashion lover. She's healthy, stylish, connected, and the go-to woman in her circle of friends. On the other hand, Melody's business networking component includes workshops, conferences, and city guides to help women entrepreneurs grow their businesses and attract new customers. The profile for the ideal CRAVE business owner is a woman in her forties, doing her own thing, and following her passion—be it jewelry making, building websites, or expanding a local boutique chain. For her, lifestyle is more important than money, and she wants to control her life and be her own boss.

Both audience groups earn a household income upwards of $75,000 per year. "The CRAVE brand is all about celebrating independent and stylish women who are doing cool things in every city we're in," says Melody. "It's about creating connections and fostering innovation among women. We want to bring women-owned businesses and their desired customers together to learn, connect, and inspire."

Melody's brand combines style, powerful femininity, innovation, and community and guides each of her decisions, including which markets to enter, how to promote her company, and how she selects women-owned businesses for the city guides. "We stick with urban areas where lots of style and inspiration can be found. We also never do broad ads because our brand is all about connections and word of mouth," she says. "CRAVE is the secret that the most stylish and successful women share with their girlfriends. If we did mainstream ads, we would lose that brand essence and we wouldn't attract the independent woman we seek who wants to be the first to discover a unique find."

This strong brand definition means CRAVE stays away from big conferences and events where other women's groups may be. Most of their promotion comes from word of mouth, email marketing, press coverage, and extensive use of social media to get the buzz going.

///

Determining Your Marketing Plan

When putting together your marketing plan, it's important to know where your ideal buying audience goes. Try to be in those places. And so you don't lose your sanity trying to promote and advertise everywhere, go deep rather than broad. By this I mean identify a few key publications, websites, or events that are exactly the right fit for you and create an integrated marketing package with each ad sales rep. Most small businesses don't have the budget to do a lot of advertising and marketing in every single place their ideal customer might be. So pick a few partners and try to do as much as you can with each one, versus a one-time shot across many different vehicles.

Whitney Keyes is a professor, marketing consultant, and author who advises small business owners around the world on how to streamline their marketing plans. The U.S. State Department has even sent her to developing countries to run workshops with budding entrepreneurs. In her book, *Propel: Five Ways to Amp Up Your Marketing and Accelerate Business* (Career Press), one of her main points is to keep things simple.

"Most entrepreneurs and business managers have no problem coming up with great ideas, but when it's time to turn that into an actionable plan, their eyes glaze over," Whitney says. "The trick is not to get overwhelmed. Keep things as straightforward and streamlined as possible."

What is the one thing you can do to boost and brand your business *right now* that is at your fingertips? Whitney advises building a simple marketing plan using the classic Five Ws and One H taught in journalism classes—*What, Who, Where, When, Why*— and add in one more *How*. For example:

- *WHAT needs to get done?* We need to design a logo for maximum brand awareness and consistency.

- *WHO will do it?* We can either hire a great designer or do it in-house.

- *WHERE will I do/use this?* We need the logo for our website, business cards, and stationery, plus we have an event coming up and need to create signage and printed marketing materials.

- *WHEN is the deadline?* We need the logo designed by March 1 so that we have time to create all our materials for a May 1 launch.

- *HOW much will it cost?* What is my budget for this? If we're using an external designer, we need to get bids on the project and allocate those funds.

- *HOW will it be measured?* Don't think you can measure *every* marketing tactic? Think again! Make sure what you're spending your time and budget on is really working.

Assessing results will ensure all of these fun activities you want to do are justified in support of your business goals. Always establish some type of metric for everything you do, even for basic marketing items that the business requires that may not have immediate revenue impact. "Foundational marketing pieces need to be tracked and measured, too," says Whitney, "even if they are not meant to directly impact revenue." Are you getting more website hits, have you gauged customer reactions, is your marketing collateral being downloaded or not? Don't let yourself get stuck in a rut by saying, "We always do this" or "Everyone always has this." See what works for your business. Reassess once or twice a year and measure effectiveness to see if these tactics are still serving your purpose. Revisit and tweak even routine awareness tactics, such as your LinkedIn profile. If you need a refresher on this topic, we discussed the importance of metrics with Question 10 of the Brand Strategy exercise back in Part 2 of the book.

The Rule of Three

One way to save your marketing sanity is to follow what I call *The Rule of Three.* In a given month or quarter, depending on your budget, focus on three publications, three website partners, three events, etc. Engaging in fewer activities—but more of the right ones—will be more effective than skipping a stone across the lake and barely making a splash with each marketing vehicle.

> Engaging in fewer activities—but more of the right ones—will be more effective than skipping a stone across the lake and barely making a splash with each marketing vehicle.

For example, you might partner with a website community that fits your audience profile, and negotiate the following add-ons in your agreement:

- a dedicated email to their subscriber list
- exposure at an event or webcast they're sponsoring
- online ads in different forums over a three- or six-month period, rather than just a one-time ad
- permission to write an article or blog post on a brand-related topic

Many website owners and ad sales reps are delighted to get creative and you can put a multitouch marketing program in place to get your brand promise in front of the right people multiple times and in multiple ways.

Magazines, professional organizations, radio stations, TV shows, websites, and events all have their own brand promise and attract certain audiences. If you know your brand well, you can confidently decide which ones align with your best possible customers, your values, and your benefits.

The same holds true for deciding on partners. Yes, some distribution partners may give you access to millions of people you'd never be able to reach. But if none of those people will buy from you or be attracted to your brand promise, then that is just money and energy down the drain. You only want to partner with firms that won't downgrade your brand or get you in front of people who won't buy from you. You can see an example of using brand to guide distribution decisions in DRY Soda's Brand at Work case study that follows.

Brand at Work: DRY Soda Company

A strong Brand Strategy doesn't remain stagnant—it evolves and adapts to changing demands and dynamics, while remaining close to its roots. Sharelle Klaus, founder and CEO of DRY Soda Company (Drysoda.com), evolved her strategy while staying true to her mission of creating a new soda category. Sharelle saw a market need for a better soda, made with better ingredients.

Sharelle wanted to create a beverage that was all-natural, caffeine-free, low in sugar, and made with the highest quality ingredients—a beverage that was perfect to sip on its own, pair with a great meal, or mix in a delicious cocktail. With a passion for all things culinary, she looked to her garden for flavors she loved and created DRY's initial four flavors.

Today DRY Soda is available in eleven flavors: blood orange, ginger, vanilla bean, apple, cherry, rhubarb, lavender, juniper berry, cucumber, wild lime and pear. DRY's brand is modern, all-natural, well-designed, and engages the consumer. The brand is conveyed through gorgeous packaging, including bottles and new slim cans; a simple, modern visual identity; and the fact that DRY is found at a variety of traditional and natural retail stores, restaurants, cafes, bars, hotels, and sampling events.

During the first years, as the brand grew, DRY protected its brand by carefully choosing quality distribution partners. Initially, they didn't want to mass market it in any way. However, consumer beverage choices are changing and wellness has become a bigger priority to everyone, not just the premium market. People are cutting down on sugar, and First Lady Michelle Obama unveiled an initiative to fight childhood obesity. The *New England Journal of Medicine* asked soda companies to lower their sweetness level, and DRY Soda was the only one that met the requirement. In keeping with the brand positioning as a "better-for-you soda company," DRY evolved the strategy to meet consumers where they are today. So DRY expanded the flavor choices to include more mainstream preferences, decreased the price point to stay competitive, launched several flavors in slim cans, and opened up more distribution channels.

DRY is staying true to the brand by continuing to choose distribution partners with great care. Partners are educated on DRY's brand values and customer promises. As new market distribution is opened, DRY is finding which brand levers work in different markets. But DRY stays on course to the original brand values of all-natural, less sweet, better for you, and well-designed in order to maintain a relationship with the early-adopter consumers.

"We still need to build the brand customer by customer, even though we're expanding our reach," says Sharelle. "We always want any new consumer's first experience with DRY to be consistent with the brand, and you tell your brand story by where people can find you. We build our brand region by region, so people can develop strong emotional attachments, and that approach influences how we roll out the product in each new market." DRY Soda can be found throughout the United States and Canada and in limited international distribution.

Make Room for Content Marketing

These days, there's more to your marketing plan compared to a traditional plan even ten years ago. In today's marketing-overload world, most people don't want the hard sell. People are jaded by pushy sales tactics and fatigued by the hard sell coming at them every single day. In order to cut through the clutter, your marketing plans need to incorporate new ways of thinking. Jay Baer is a social media consultant and author of the best–selling book, *Youtility* (Portfolio). He educates and delights thousands of people every day through his blog, podcasts, and email newsletters from Convince and Convert, his consulting firm. If anyone is an expert in how to engage prospects and customers in new ways, it's Jay. "People recognize that the marketing and advertising approaches of yesteryear are no longer as effective as they used to be," he says. "We don't consume media in the same ways we did in the past. So as marketers, what we used to do doesn't work. There's got to be a different way."

You know this is true for yourself. You most likely are not consuming content the same way you used to either, so why shouldn't this be true for your audience as well?

Today's marketing is all about creating a relationship with your target customer, building a community, and creating that irresistible brand. This is where *content marketing* comes in.

Content marketing is a buzz phrase that's been bandied about as the new way to reach customers. But what does it mean and how can you create it, share it, and ensure it achieves your goals?

According to Ann Handley, chief content officer of MarketingProfs.com and co-author of *Content Rules: How to Create Killer Blogs, Podcasts, Videos, Ebooks (and More) That Engage Customers and Ignite Your Business* (Wiley), engaging in content marketing means to consistently create and share information that is packed with utility, seeded with inspiration, and is honestly empathetic to attract customers to you.

Now that you have identified your target ideal client or customer in your Brand Strategy, you need to be specific in what you put out into the world with your brand's voice, spin, and perspective. "You want to reach the person who has a problem that your business can solve," says Ann. "That means your content should anticipate what questions your customers have, and answer them. Create content centered on these questions: What problems can we solve for people searching for us? What questions can we answer? How can we help them do something? How can we create content that helps people with a problem? How can we be there in a moment of need?"

While this may seem overwhelming, it's about making sure that the messaging and content you create is relevant and interesting to your audience, based on your Brand Strategy. Doing so ensures you don't spend a lot of cycles creating marketing that is useless to them and yields no results for you.

Content has always been part of the marketing mix. When you create advertising, sales copy, or free brochures, it's technically all content. But we've evolved beyond mere sales pitching to offering true value to our customers. So why is content such a big deal for businesses or organizations today? Ann believes that three recent developments have made it especially crucial.

First, technology has evolved, eliminating the publishing gatekeepers. "You once needed a large budget and access to a printing press to create and distribute content on a large scale, or you had to buy access to an audience," says Ann. Now you can be your own publisher by editing videos to share on YouTube or writing blog articles in order to connect with people you want to reach. No gatekeeper holding you back. And don't forget how important such fresh, consistent content is to build awareness online. This content enables you to be found via Google or social media recommendations to build your brand awareness in ways never before possible on such scale.

Second, content marketing is necessary because social media is now a daily part of our lives. "It's not just about creating content that will allow you to be found online," says Ann. Instead, you're tasked with creating content that's worth sharing, because your updates are competing on social media platforms with your audience's friends and family. There's no point in using social media as an engagement channel if you have nothing to say or offer. It can't just be all sales messages all the time. "That means your content has to be really good in order to get my attention, and it has to be valuable: It has to entertain me, delight me, or inform me."

Third, and most importantly, content marketing is required to adapt to changing consumer behavior. "It used to be that your sales force was on the front lines," says Ann. "But now that role is being filled by the Internet; customers are online, searching for answers and resources and asking for recommendations on Facebook, LinkedIn, and Twitter." Content marketing enables you to show up to the party with the good beer. This creates a virtual sales force of non-employees that are just as, if not more than, influential in the purchase decisions of their friends and family. And review sites and apps like Yelp, Urbanspoon, and TripAdvisor have proven that even strangers can influence our buying habits.

Crafting a Content Marketing Plan

Okay, so you recognize the need for good content marketing to stay active in social media, gain the trust of prospects, and build a loyal brand following. How do you go about creating a plan?

Ann Handley recommends the following thought process to put together your content marketing plan:

First, figure out where your customers are. Do they hang out online? Or are they mostly offline? Do they read certain blogs, sites, or are they active on social networks like Twitter, Facebook, LinkedIn, or Instagram? Where do they get their information? Review sites? Friends and family? Brand content?

How can you figure this out? ASK THEM. Poll your existing customers, or people like your target customers if you're just starting out. You can easily do this with a free online survey tool like Survey Monkey or something similar. Or you could ask them in a face-to-face informal focus group, by email, or simply by picking up the phone and calling them. If your business is currently up and running, can you include a survey after each purchase or project? Ann advises, "Mapping where your customers are helps to define what you'll create and where."

Next, what kind of content works best based on what you now know about these people? "If you have a socially savvy audience, for example, you might create a blog and robust Facebook page," says Ann. This is where you should also consider what you enjoy doing, or you'll never stick with it. Are you a gifted writer? Or are you better at talking and presenting information? If it is the former, a weekly blog or informational e-book may work best. If the latter, perhaps a weekly podcast on topics relevant to your audience suits you. Determining what works best will also help you map out frequency and timing. For example, you don't want to post more than one or two Facebook posts a day on your brand's page. You don't want to create a new e-book for download every week when one every quarter will do. If you do weekly videos, you can film them all in one day and schedule them out. Remember, think about the Rule of Three we discussed earlier and keep your marketing activity plan simple and focused. Once you know the content and channels you're targeting, you can build a content marketing plan or editorial calendar to guide what you need to create and when—and to create assets well in advance of when you'll actually post them live.

Finally, create content that delights. "Create content that your customers will thank you for," says Ann. "Don't just talk about your products. Focus on being a source to your prospects and buyers. Make your customer the hero of your story!" This is the best way to ensure that when they *are* ready to buy, they will think of you first.

Crafting great content can create a loyal following and shape the brand as it grows—especially if you are a blogger and starting a business is not your intention. The following Brand at Work case study on Happy Herbivore is a perfect example.

Brand at Work: Happy Herbivore

Can you stumble upon your brand as you go, simply by creating great content? You bet. When Lindsay S. Nixon decided to start blogging on a whim a few years ago, she never in her wildest dreams thought it would springboard into a book, let alone a company with a strong brand and profitable programs. As an author and CEO of Happy Herbivore Inc. (Happyherbivore.com), Lindsay is dedicated to helping people live better and eat healthy, plant-based foods. She writes cookbooks and the company offers seven-day meal plans, a three-day reboot, a ten-day cleanse immersion, and most recently, an entrepreneurship class.

Even without a formal brand strategy at first, her brand now shines as one that is inclusive, happy, and honest. But what she always had was a strong mission statement: both for herself personally and for her business. This statement served as her early version of a Brand Strategy. "Whenever I'm faced with an opportunity, I ask whether it furthers my mission," says Lindsay. "If I have a problem or need to make a tough decision, I always go back to my mission statement."

Lindsay admits that she didn't start out with a clear vision for her business because she never intended to build one. "It just sort of happened out of my own personal passions. If I had a strong Brand Strategy and mission from the get-go, I could have saved myself so much time and energy. Now, I tell my business-class students that they have to write their mission statement and learn from my missteps. Before anything else, they have to know where they are going!"

Lindsay started off by simply meeting a need in the market. "I started blogging because no one was talking about what I was interested in, so I decided to do it in case there was someone else out there like me. Later on I realized how lucky that was—how this specific 'unique selling proposition' [USP] helped me stand out and be successful later. Now I'm known for it."

The company does not pay for marketing or advertising. Given the company's roots as a blog, they simply adopted a content marketing strategy of publishing free, useful content that delights their audience. "Our products speak for themselves and our customers pass it along. No amount of marketing is as good as word of mouth. You just can't buy that kind of solid publicity."

Clearly her strategy is working. As of this publication date, Happy Herbivore has about 72,000 Facebook fans and over 27,000 Twitter followers. Lindsay has sold close to 200,000 cookbooks (in less than two years) and about 8 million people have visited the blog in the past year. And they've expanded the brand into other areas, including Getmealplans.com and Rebootcleanse911.com. Because of Lindsay's "accidental entrepreneur" success, she's also launched an entrepreneurship class to share what she's learned (Exitstrategyschool.com).

Creating Compelling Content: Being Human

I once heard a conference speaker, who had successfully increased her company's blog visits one hundredfold, share this advice: your content must make people laugh, cry, or fume if you want it to be engaging. While true, I'd also add that it should be informative and valuable. And most importantly, everything you create should be wrapped in your brand voice and personality. This is where your Brand Strategy will prove useful in ensuring all your content is giving your audience a consistent experience. You wouldn't want to spend time and energy crafting a fun, quirky, playful brand and attracting people who dig that sort of thing—and then deliver boring, dry, severe content, would you?

Being human matters as well. My dream is that someday soon, jargon-filled websites and brochures will be a thing of the past, and that all content will sound like real humans speaking to each other. This is especially frustrating with business-to-business brands that think they need to talk or act a certain way. True, your Brand Strategy needs to go a bit native to appeal to your target ideal customers. But there's a huge difference between being professional and serious to establish credibility, and meaningless blather.

Blogger and writer Sarah Von Bargen (Sarahvonbargen.com) is a trusted partner of mine in helping craft clients' brand messaging, sales copy, and website content. She's also a gifted content marketing consultant for solopreneurs and small organizations. Her advice for both sales copy as well as content marketing? "Remove jargon and corporate slang from your copy," she advises. "It rubs people the wrong way and makes you and your company hard to relate to. Speak to your readers and customers the way you'd speak to a friend—with warmth and humor." Again, this doesn't mean you can't speak the accepted language of your industry or target demographic. Just remember to be human and you'll be all right.

Creating Compelling Content: Finding the Time

You may be thinking, "This is all great, but when am I going to find the time to create all of this? I'm barely keeping my head above water now with the marketing basics!" Once you create a content marketing plan or editorial calendar, it's much easier to outsource. You don't have to do all the work yourself! Maybe you allow guest writers to blog for you twice a month. Perhaps your customers might get excited about creating videos you can post on your Facebook page if you make a contest out of it. Or you can work with a complementary business partner targeting a similar audience with a different offering to work with you on hosting a podcast. Ask customers to enter a twenty-five-word essay contest and post the best entries. And remember, college interns in communications, marketing, or video production are always looking for ways to learn and grow!

All of this is easier to do if you first have a game plan. Then you can figure out how to divide and conquer. You can easily create one in Excel: you don't have to use any fancy apps or complicated processes. Jay Baer, the social media consultant and author we heard from earlier, says, "The content planning process is more about the wizard than the wand being used!" It does help, however, to have someone overseeing the process and ensuring it all gets done. This could be an intern, a part-time resource, or a full-time consultant or employee.

Finally, beware of perfection. Jay warns that "Polish is the enemy of scale. Always. We are fundamentally off-track right now, holding up on a pedestal the amazing, super-polished e-book, webinar, white paper. Production value is highly praised in TV and I get it, but it's not scalable." Rather than shining that diamond to super-awesome perfection only once per quarter, the future is all about consistent and frequent content in both polished and unpolished forms. "You may have employees on the frontlines with amazing customer service stories or fun personalities," says Jay. "Or customers who send you thank-you emails. You have sources you don't even think of as content—use them!"

Do I Really Need a Blog?

Blogging is just one aspect of content marketing. But nothing strikes more fear in clients than when I suggest they start a blog. The excuses usually include the following:

"I don't have time."

"I hate writing."

"How can I possibly write a post every single week about [insert name or product or service here]?"

As Sarah Von Bargen advises, "Nobody *has* to do anything, but blogging is a cheap and relatively easy way to connect with thousands of potential customers and boost your SEO so your content shows up in searches more often than your competition's."

If time is an issue, pick a rate of frequency that's easy for you to start. Most blog platforms have tools to schedule your posts in advance, so you can bang out multiple posts in one sitting and not worry about it for a while. No one says you have to post every day or even twice a week. For some people and audiences this could work, but for you, time or resources might be an issue—and heck, maybe people don't want to hear from you every single day! No matter what you decide, the key is to stay consistent. You don't want a blog that hasn't been updated in months, and you want to set expectations with your audience so they get trained to check back at the same intervals.

If writing is not your thing, hire a college intern or freelance writer to help you. Or you can use the blog for other types of media, as Ann Handley suggested earlier: Promote a podcast with just a short written introduction. Film a video and post it to your blog. Use images, pictures, simple web link round-up lists, or video interviews with experts in whom your audience may be interested. It's not always just about the written word.

Coming up blank about what to talk about? Jay Baer suggests you focus on creating content that is overtly useful. This could include content that isn't even directly about your products or services but closely related. This is not only more interesting than fifty-two posts on luggage, if that's what you sell, but what do your target buyers also care about and need? Most likely such topics as travel, organization, time management, top-ten best airline lounges, most photographed tourist sites on Instagram, or how vegan leather is made. You want to become a resource destination to build your brand cache and credibility. "It's never just about your product or service," says Jay. "That's merely a means to an end."

What do they really want and need? Go back to your ideal-customer profiles you created—look into their lives, interests, fears. Address those. They will see you more as a trusted resource who "gets" them, than if you just blather on about features and functions. Sarah Von Bargen also suggests making a list of the most common questions you get from clients and customers. Each question could be a new blog post or content marketing idea.

Build Your Own Tribe

There may be thousands or millions (or billions) of ideal customers out there who can benefit from your products or services. But you are a small organization—where is the lowest-hanging fruit that will be easiest for you to engage, inform, and delight with all this great new content you're creating? That's where building your own tribe comes in.

You can spend endless dollars paying to reach your audience through other people or organizations: buying ads, sponsoring events, sending out email campaigns to rental lists. But the best way to activate an audience that's primed to hear what you have to say is to build *your own* tribe.

Start collecting email addresses and building your own proprietary email list. These are people who will opt-in and raise their hand to hear more from you. This is the single most valuable thing you can do to grow your business. Mind you, not all of these people may be customers—yet. That's the point. They are taking the first step to know, like, and trust you, and when it comes time to plunk down cash to meet their needs, they will think of you first. This is often known as *lead nurturing* but I prefer to call it *tribe building*.

DJ Waldow is an email expert and digital marketing evangelist at Marketo, a marketing-automation company. He blogs about all things email marketing at Marketo's blog (blog.marketo.com/blog/author/dj-waldow). Contrary to what many people believe, email marketing is still one of the best ways to engage an audience. "More than ever, it's harder and harder to get people's attention," says DJ. "Certain studies show that people are exposed to over three hundred media messages every day, but of those, only 2 percent are seen or remembered. These days, there are too many distractions across all forms of media. You have to make sure people know who you are first and that they trust you. Social media content just goes by, whereas email captures someone specifically for *you* and your brand."

But if your mom and your significant other are the only ones on your email list, how can you go about building it? Sign up for an email automation service, such as MailChimp, Emma, Constant Contact, AWeber, Infusionsoft, Marketo, ExactTarget, or others, and install their sign-up widget on your website to start collecting names as soon as possible. Make sure it's placed above the web page fold so people can see it without scrolling down the page and offer them an incentive to sign up—perhaps a white paper, discounted shipping, a free gift, or a podcast (review the content marketing sections above).

Whenever you do events, make sure you have a sign-up sheet, even if it's old-fashioned pen and paper, for people to join your list. And reach out to your current customers and fans to ensure they join your list as well. DJ says the key to brand building is all in how you are growing your email list. "Are you setting expectations up-front and giving people a reason to sign up? Make it obvious and clear and easy for people to sign up for your list." One of the biggest mistakes organizations make is that they don't think about growing this list until it's too late. You can't build it when you're ready to promote something; you have to have it in place before you do. "You can't build a strong email list overnight," warns DJ. "You have to be growing it all along and communicating relevant, engaging, and compelling content with those people. Then when you launch a funding project on Kickstarter or roll out a new promotion, your audience is already there. List building should come before you need it, not after!"

Building your own email list ensures you have a captive audience for all that juicy content you're creating. These are the people who will share the most compelling content on *their* social media networks, exponentially expanding your reach and increasing word of mouth better than a lone passing Tweet from you ever could. Personally, I have seen the power in my own business of sharing blog posts with my email list first and watching as those brand advocates spread the word for me, rather than doing all the heavy lifting myself!

Your email list is not just for promoting your goods and services. People will soon tire of simply getting ads in their inbox. As we discussed in the content marketing sections above, it's about being a trusted resource and offering a steady stream of compelling content that is both useful and entertaining. This email tribe will be your primary focus for offering stellar content and resources and only then will they be open to hearing about your latest and greatest products and services. A good rule of thumb: stick to 80 percent valuable content and 20 percent sales messages.

Getting Social

Now that you've created a content marketing plan and have assets to share, it's time to expand beyond your website and your own opt-in tribe. This is where social media comes into play. But if you're starting from ground zero, it can be tough to figure out into which social media pool to dive.

Amy Schmittauer is president of Vlog Boss Studios, a digital marketing agency with a focus on video content strategy. But she is best recognized for her work on the marketing lifestyle video blog Savvy Sexy Social (Savvysexysocial.com). Amy makes navigating the social media rapids easy and affordable, with lots of quick tips and DIY advice. She advises that you don't even think about diving into social media without your Brand Strategy firmly in place. "Social media is not a Brand Strategy. It's not even your marketing strategy," she says. "It's not the 'be all, end all' and you still need to look at and leverage other channels if it makes sense. You keep hearing things like 'print and radio are dying.' Well, they're not. They are still relevant for certain brands and audiences. It depends on the ROI you are looking for."

If you've determined that social media needs to be a part of your marketing mix to reach and influence the right audience, how can you figure out which platforms should be part of your social media plan?

The first step to an effective plan is to identify your ideal customer. We already talked about this as the single most important aspect of your Brand Strategy, which is why thinking through your Brand Strategy before you do anything is so useful. "There is no way to get started in social media without knowing for whom your brand personality, products, or services are a good fit," says Amy. "Be clear. If you don't know this, you're done."

The next step is to create a short list based on where that target audience is most likely to be. There are some broad-brush usage patterns out there. For example, if you have a "manly" brand targeting thrill-seeking men, Pinterest may not be your scene, as it tends to attract more women. Right now, it looks like the teen community is pulling away from Facebook and using platforms with more privacy, such as Snapchat, WhatsApp, and Twitter (as of the publication of this book). Usage patterns evolve, so make sure you are constantly staying abreast of industry sources such as Social Media Today, MarketingProfs, or Mashable, to name a few.

The third step is to simply *listen.* Spend an hour on each platform where you suspect you will find your target audience and find out what people are talking about. What are they sharing? To what do they respond? Spend time note-taking. Amy suggests using Search functions for keywords, phrases, or hashtags in your industry. For example, she cites travel businesses who monitor phrases such as "I want to fly to..." or "Can't wait to go to Florida!" on Twitter so they can find the conversations out there and respond with helpful tips or amusing interactions. Some even monitor social media to find out who is experiencing flight delays, and then reach out with a human touch to build their brand!

Once you pick two or three platforms in which you should invest time and energy, the final step is to share compelling content so you can build and engage your community. "If you can engage those people who like and need you consistently and often, you'll never have to pay for advertising," says Amy. Keep up your relationship with them. Don't ever let a page or account just sit there! This is why it's so important to be ready with a strong Brand Strategy before you embark on social media. "If you wait to get on a social network only when you're ready to commit full steam ahead, rather than randomly posting here and there, you can start consistent engagement from Day One and you'll succeed," advises Amy. "This helps you in the long run so you don't have to artificially 'bump up' engagement by paying to promote every single post. While there is a time and a place for paying to promote content in social media, it's the organic engagement you're after to save you time and money."

As of this book's publication, Amy advises, "Twitter is the new Facebook in terms of what you have to have so you may want to always include it in your mix." The Facebook algorithm changes all the time but Twitter lets you see trends and streams so you can jump on relevant hot topics. "Facebook doesn't make it easy to find relevant news for news streams, even though they have started to adopt hashtags. Everything is chronological, not calculated." Balance this with other channels that are prime hangouts for your audience—women on Pinterest, for example, or adults and Boomers on Facebook, etc.

Networking: Building Your Brand Online and Offline

Since brand is all about every touch point and experience people have with your organization, making connections and networking is a vital component of your brand-building strategy. Few business owners realize that networking—in-person or online—should actually be a marketing budget line item and something you schedule into your weekly plans.

While your business may be virtual and serve customers anywhere in the world, the most important source of referrals is often found in meeting people face to face. Whether you do this by attending local or regional events in your city or flying to industry conferences a few times a year, those in-person connections can build your brand most effectively.

Sandy Jones-Kaminski is chief connecting officer of Bella Domain Media (Belladomain.com). Sandy helps entrepreneurs connect online and offline. As a networking expert, she's even written a book called *I'm at a Networking Event—Now What???* (Happy About Press) mainly because she knows that too many business owners dread this vital marketing tool. ""Networking online and offline is a necessary marketing investment in your business," says Sandy. "It never has to be a waste of time. And since some events, conferences, and groups require a fee; networking should be part of your marketing budget."

In today's world, we're lucky that we have both offline and online options for networking. But it's important to use both if you want to build an irresistible brand and maximize your reach.

Online, it's important not to confuse social media marketing with social networking. "Social media marketing is much more akin to traditional marketing, in that it's trying to achieve the same thing: sales, leads, interest, and buzz," says Sandy

Social networking, however, is a different animal with different rules and outcomes. While it can be done on many of the same platforms as social media marketing (for example, LinkedIn, Twitter, and Facebook), Sandy teaches, "Social networking is about staying in touch. It's the way we make connections and the way we develop and cultivate those connections. In the past, people used a Rolodex and a phone. Then we gravitated to email as a way to stay in touch." With online social networking tools and activities, you can not only stay in touch with people you meet in person, but you have the ability to create new connections with people you'll probably never meet face-to-face. There is so much more online information available. You can research common interests with a customer or supplier before you've ever even met and have a conversation starter available at your fingertips. You can also connect with potential partners and customers who are across the globe.

This distinction between social media marketing and social networking is important to understand because both serve a purpose in your brand-building efforts. You just need to be clear about what you get from each tactic.

When engaging in social networking, you need to come at it from a place of generosity and mutual benefit, not a sales angle. Try to present yourself online as you would at an in-person event. You'd never just meet someone for the first time, shove your business card in their face, and ask them to buy what you're selling, would you? While there are some people that do this, it's not the best way to boost your brand perception! Be human and be consistent online with your brand, just as you would offline.

"You often see people present themselves one way in their website or profile, but they would never be that way in person," says Sandy. "Such inconsistency can hurt your brand. You want to authentically present you and your brand to people online the same way you would if they walked into your store or met you at a meeting." While it's true that some industries, such as finance or academia, may require a certain formality due to legal issues or government regulations, for the most part social networking is about presenting yourself as human. "You are your brand, especially if you're a solopreneur or small businesses owner," says Sandy. "Be consistent with the same voice, values, and style online as well as offline." Of course, use caution: You can't be overly familiar with someone online whom you don't know very well! That's just bad form!

You can use social networking platforms to follow up on connections you make in person to reinforce your brand. When you meet someone at an event, exchange cards and invite them to connect with you through social media. If you do this, they are more inclined to click through to your profile and learn more about your business and brand than if you'd sent an email with a website link. Make sure you take the time to create a polished profile that reflects your brand.

Why does social networking even matter when you have so much else to do? Sandy suggests that one reason is that the bigger your network, the more successful you and your brand may be perceived. "Like it or not, there is a certain cachet to how far-reaching your connections are," she says. "It connotes having success and a certain amount of resources available to you."

"Social networking simply reinforces who you are in the world," says Sandy. "The way you are in the world as a professional either supports or hurts your brand, whether we're talking about a personal or business brand. You reflect on your company. You are the brand experience. Your social interactions with people in social media—and offline as well—need to be polite, kind, thoughtful, and worded carefully." Without being intentional or making the time to consistently do this as part of your marketing, you will fall short.

Here are eight tips for achieving offline and online networking bliss:

1. **Follow up online with offline contacts:** When you meet offline, immediately connect with key contacts through online social channels, such as Twitter, LinkedIn, or Google+ to keep that connection fresh and avoid spamming. "Don't wait too long," cautions Sandy, "Do this within forty-eight hours. If you're at a conference, as tired as you might be at end of day, it's smart to do this as soon as you can so the connection is fresh in both of your minds."

2. **Personalize the note:** Do not send invitations to connect on a social channel without personalizing the message. Say something meaningful! Remind them how you met or compliment them on their website. "Take this opportunity to make that connection deeper," says Sandy. Some social networks, like LinkedIn, require you to have an email to connect. If you don't have their email, you can mark them as a "Friend," but again, make sure you personalize the message and add a P.S. to apologize for playing the "Friend" card.

3. **Give before you get:** Think about a connection you can make for this person that benefits them. Surely there is someone you know who might make a good client, partner, or mentor. Be generous and share. "Some people are better at connecting dots than others. It's like they maintain a mental map in their brains," says Sandy. "If you're not naturally like this, after you learn about their professional or personal

interests, stop and think about anyone you know who might benefit from knowing them. Not leads, not prospects, just *knowing* them." Connect them over email with a mini-intro for each person about why you think they might be interested in connecting with the other person.

4. **Acknowledge people who acknowledge you:** Try to acknowledge @mentions or Comments if you can, especially those on a blog post or group discussion you've started in social media. "It's super easy to 'Like' a comment they've posted or to retweet something they had to say. It shows you are paying attention—and it takes only seconds, so no excuses!" says Sandy.

5. **Participate in online groups:** Many social media platforms such as LinkedIn or Facebook offer online groups. Try different groups on for size and see which ones fit. "Treat them like a coat you'd return to Nordstrom," says Sandy. "If you don't like it, you can leave the group." How do you try groups on? First, just listen. "Don't feel you have to start posting or commenting right away," says Sandy. "Just get a feel for the tone and vibe of the group. What discussions are taking place? Are they more personal in nature? Funny? Serious?" Search for topics that are relevant to you within each group to see if those discussions are happening. For example, Sandy worked with a post-traumatic stress disorder (PTSD) psychotherapist who was interested in finding LinkedIn groups that were relevant to her business. Once she found a few groups that looked like good possibilities, she typed in "PTSD" to see if people were talking about the topic within the group. She then cherry-picked relevant discussions, reviewed them, and decided if she wanted to comment or contribute. "It's a good idea to comment

with a link to support the person's discussion. This helps supports their expertise, showcases your own insights, and reflects on your brand without selling!" notes Sandy.

6. **Follow experts and other thought-leaders:** With many social media channels, you can follow people to whom you are not linked, whether they are famous or not. "These influencers can give you a steady stream of content that you can share with your groups and contacts," says Sandy.

7. **Don't join too many peer groups:** This is true for both online and offline networking. While it's important to network with peers, remember not to join too many groups. You will just end up talking to your competition! "You need to make sure you are in a few industry or peer groups for collaboration and referrals," advises Sandy. "But be sure you're also engaging in groups targeting your prospects and ideal customers." This is a great way to hear about what challenges they face that you may solve, plus it's a prime opportunity to showcase your brand each time you contribute.

8. **Stay clear and true to your brand, and the right people will find *you*:** Staying active in group conversations is a great way to get your name out there so that reporters, bloggers, and other media influentials in your space can find you. And if they are in your groups, be sure to comment on their posts as well. "If there is a reporter that covers your industry and you're not ready to pitch them quite yet, start following them and when they post, be sure to comment or contribute in a relevant way," says Sandy. "If your name keeps showing up on their posts, they will notice. And then it's not such a cold call when you contact them."

As with any other part of your brand-building plan, you must recognize the need to put in networking time. This will be valuable time you bill to yourself. "Networking, whether online or offline, isn't wasting time," says Sandy. "It's time spent investing in your business and brand." While it's a different form of marketing, networking reinforces your personal and professional brand. Remember, when you work for yourself or a small organization, you don't have a million-dollar budget behind you to promote the brand. *You are the brand.*

> Remember, when you work for yourself or a small organization, you don't have a million-dollar budget behind you to promote the brand. *You are the brand.*

Networking isn't just about what that person can do for you at this moment in time, but about how you can help them. "While someone may not be a direct prospect now, they likely know someone who is," advises Sandy. More often than not, sharing interesting articles, events, or other helpful information helps build a true rapport. The connection builds real depth because when you support what they are doing, you are most likely to be the first business to come to mind when someone they know needs what you've got to offer.

For those of you rolling your eyes at the thought of making idle luncheon chitchat or tooting your own horn a bit, consider this: "You have to trust that your network is going to be supportive of you to a certain degree," says Sandy. "A reasonable amount of necessary self-promotion is tolerated and supported. Most of your peers understand that if you don't get out there and promote your own brand, who else is going to do it?" The key is to avoid being overly aggressive or too braggy.

"Networking is a bit like taxes," explains Sandy. "You have to pay them, but unlike taxes, building a network gives back and benefits you and your brand." With people to help shoulder the burden of self-promotion, you won't have to do it all alone.

Remember, networking is a business expense. You have to do 80 percent of the work but if you build and nurture a strong network, it can and will help you with the other 20 percent.

Operationalizing Your Brand

So we've seen how brand can inform your visual elements, messaging elements, and marketing tactics. We've seen the role it plays in informing your social media and content marketing strategy. But brand can do even more for your business if you let it. Since brand is grounded in your promise to customers, you need to live your brand in everything you do. This means your company operations as well. Remember, we've talked about brand being conveyed not only visually and verbally but also through experience. Now we'll discuss this "experiential" component. If you're going to talk the talk, you need to walk the walk. Brand as a promise and philosophy should influence your organization inside and out—through internal procedures, production processes, partner programs, hiring practices, and even your office and store décor.

> Brand as a promise and philosophy should influence your organization inside and out—through internal procedures, production processes, partner programs, hiring practices, and even your office and store décor.

Think about a company that promises customer service as their first priority. All their ads communicate personalized service and attention. Their website design and colors are warm and inviting. The tagline even says something like "Customers First." Yet when you call their customer service line, you enter a voicemail maze from hell that never gets you to a live person and doesn't help answer your question. Worse, when you finally get to an option to "Speak to an operator," you're put on hold with a wait time of ten minutes while being forced to listen to an automated message claiming, "Your call is important to us." Sound familiar? This is because the brand promise made by the marketing department isn't knitted into the DNA of how the company does business. Somehow the folks in charge of the customer service line weren't included in the branding process to see how their structure, processes—and even the automated technology they may have picked—contributes to the overall brand promise. So the company has an identity crisis. They've told me customers are number one in everything they say, but my experience proves otherwise.

This is what happens when companies think branding is only the marketing department's responsibility. If brand as we've defined it is indeed the sum total of all the customers' experiences, ads they've seen, messages they've heard, and even colors or designs that have subconsciously influenced their perception, then . . .

Branding is everyone's responsibility in the organization. It starts at the top, but every group from sales to customer service to fulfillment to field operations must understand how the work they do impacts the brand promise. If they can see this, they can begin creating better processes and policies for their own departments that add to the customer experience, in ways both small and large.

> Branding is *everyone's* responsibility in the organization.

For example, if a software business tries to tell me they're trustworthy, stable, and work with high-caliber Fortune 1000 companies, then the accounting department needs to know and own this. Why? Because if I'm a vendor working with that software company and I can't get my invoices paid on time, how will I perceive the company? Vendors within the same industry often work with other companies in that industry, and people talk. Rumors can start flying about your financial viability, the health of your business, and the value of your word. Vendor relations have as important a role to play in branding as do customer experiences. Word gets around, people talk, and pretty soon you'll be dealing with a sullied reputation. I've worked with a few start-up firms who thought it was fine to delay vendor payments by months and months, while promising customers that they were stable and could deliver immediate value. But we all know how small the world can be, and how brand inconsistency across the organization can actually turn customers away. In the following Brand at Work case study, we see how Jeni's Splendid Ice Creams built their irresistible brand by walking their talk through employee actions, product quality, and customer delight.

\\\

Brand at Work: Jeni's Splendid Ice Creams

"We are defined by what we do, not what we say we will do." This is the mantra of Jeni Britton Bauer, president, chief creative officer, founder, and ice cream maker at Jeni's Splendid Ice Creams (Jenis.com) based in Columbus, Ohio. Jeni's brand promise is to make the best ice creams imaginable for their large and ever-growing fan base across the country. While that sounds good on paper, Jeni's actually puts their money where their mouth is: Their ice creams are made by hand from scratch with fairly-traded local, regional, and internationally sourced or produced ingredients and with a base of grass-pastured milk.

"When you place a spoonful of ice cream on your tongue, it will be the most luscious, buttery, flavorful, and delicious ice cream you're ever had," promises Jeni. With scoop shops in four states and distribution at specialty food stores around the country, they are delighting customers coast to coast.

Jeni's knows that nothing conveys a brand promise quite like the actual customer experience. In the early days, there was no logo and the store signage consisted of a small *Jeni's Splendid Ice Creams* sign printed in black on an 11x17-inch sheet of paper. Hanging from the shop rafters with neon orange-tipped plastic gray clips, the sign "could not be further from cool!" says Jeni.

In addition to making the best quality product, the company creates an in-store atmosphere to make customers feel welcomed, celebrated, and inspired. They live by the brand attributes of goodwill, civility, and creativity. Flavors change constantly and follow the season, pop culture, history, art—or even just capricious whim.

Jeni believes it's far more important to be a company that inspires people's trust, and to put your name on the company, so that you are never tempted to cut corners. "Your reputation *is* your brand, but you have to earn it."

To that end, the company lives their brand inside and out. "We will never compromise who we are or what we make for the sake of sales or anything else under the sun. Our external brand is an exact reflection of our internal culture."

The frontline team who serves ice cream in their stores are all required to ace a test whenever new flavors come out. They can't work the line until they can recite every ingredient's provenance, exactly how it was sourced or made, and each back-kitchen process that brought it to life.

Delivery drivers are instructed to be "superheroes." They are often seen in uniform picking up trash instead of walking over it. When the tornadoes hit central Illinois in November 2013, they immediately drove the truck down from Chicago, brought water and supplies, and helped clean up for several days. In Nashville, drivers saw a car on fire and pulled the driver to safety.

As a result of making the brand personal and creating a magical and fun environment, the company has had little need for advertising (unless they are supporting a good cause, of course). They crush their competition on social media, delighting and engaging tens of thousands of rabid fans, and lines form around the block to get a taste—even on cold winter days.

Jeni is humble about how her brand became irresistible. "It was all intact from the beginning. We just wanted to make this beautiful ice cream and serve it in a welcoming environment. We wanted to do good things. Be good citizens. I would say it's personal more than intentional, though it is that, too. More than anything, I think we just want to have fun and be a part of something magical and real, not a marketing plan. Just like your personal reputation, a strong brand can't be faked or forced. When you make promises, you have to deliver. If you don't, then you may as well go home."

Little Things Mean a Lot: Delighting Your Customers

Even the smallest customer interactions are opportunities to solidify your brand in their minds. Thinking through every touchpoint the customer has with you is a great way to find those tiny moments that can make you buzz-worthy. Companies that live their brand inside and out do this well.

> Even the smallest customer interactions are opportunities to solidify your brand in their minds.

Customers don't just see your ads, your website, or your office. What if you send them emails? Do you have an interesting email signature that showcases your logo and tagline, along with providing links to promotions or website pages? If you've won any awards, can you tout them in your email signature to reinforce your image as a great company with which to do business? If your brand has a playful attitude, can you word your automated emails in fun, fresh, or irreverent ways?

What about your office phone or customer service lines? How do employees answer the phone? If you run a beauty salon, does your receptionist simply say, "Jennifer speaking," or could she say something like, "This is Jennifer. How can we make you feel fabulous today?" Even your voicemail message can be carefully worded, or you can choose telephone on-hold music that aligns with your brand. Years ago, I loved working at Discovery Communications, owners of The Discovery Channel, TLC, Animal Planet, and other great networks. If you called and were placed on hold, you'd enjoy African tribal rhythms or some other world music. This was actually fun for customers and partners, and the music was exactly what you'd expect Discovery to play, in keeping with their brand image. Yes, they could have done nothing and let boring easy-listening music assault your ears, but they chose to use that tiny interaction as a way to further the Discovery experience. The best restaurants often hire music and lighting consultants to ensure just the right brand vibe is conveyed through each of the five senses, not just the food's taste or the waitstaff's service. The following Brand at Work case study shows how brand is used to differentiate one business in a look-alike industry, and how Dr. Jaffe conveys her brand through every possible customer touchpoint, great or small.

\\\

Brand at Work:
Lemon-Aid Counseling

Psychotherapy is not an industry known for innovative branding, but Dr. Jaelline Jaffe, PhD, is out to change that. Practicing since 1976, she started offering an eight-week Lemon-Aid course that utilized her personal experiences overcoming health issues.

Clients connected with the theme, so in 2004 she re-branded her Los Angeles practice as Lemon-Aid Counseling (LemonAidCounseling.com) and put up a website. Her mission is to help others develop a positive attitude about their life circumstances, so they can turn their life's lemons into something much sweeter. Lemon-Aid's tagline is "Living the life you have when it's not the life you wanted" and Dr. Jaffe focuses on helping people with unique medical challenges that many other therapists do not, such as tinnitus and misophonia. In a sea of look-alike therapists (especially in Los Angeles) with predictable business cards and marketing attitudes, she wanted to stand out and attract the right client. Clients who love her brand instantly feel safe, accepted, and positive. "Through my branding," she says, "I've created a filter to get responses from those who 'get it' and who connect with my down-to-earth, comforting, optimistic, and genuine style."

Dr. Jaffe lives her brand visually through her website, with its lemon tree graphics and "Make Lemonade" song link, and via her lemon tree business card logo (people at networking events quickly recognize her as The Lemonade Lady). Her office space further conveys the brand, with lemon posters and reproductions of old lemon crate labels, a needlepoint pillow (given to her by a client) with the saying *When life gives you lemons ... make lemonade!*, a lemon-painted lamp, lemon-shaped post-it pads, and lemon To-Do lists for client "homework" reminders. She experientially conveys her brand with a never-ending supply of lemon drops in the waiting room, lemonade and lemon-printed napkins for meetings, and offers client-networking gifts like lemon baskets with lemon cookies, shampoos, air fresheners, or lemon cake recipes. And she'll take potential business affiliates to lunch at local area spots like Lemonade, Lemon Moon, or Lemongrass.

To communicate her other brand values of comfort, caring, respect, peace, and a welcoming approach, Dr. Jaffe carefully designed her office and waiting room. Clients are greeted by mellow music, soft colors, low lighting, comfortable furniture, and personalized items (like toys for the kids and magazines for both men and women of all ages). Clients have told her, "I walk into the office and immediately feel held, comforted, and at peace. It's like I can take a deep breath!"

Many high-end stores will wrap your purchase in a neat and careful way that's worthy of the price you paid for that merchandise. Some of them take on the extra expense of colored tissue paper to match their visual identity. I remember Victoria's Secret used to wrap purchases in pink or black-and-white striped paper. It made you feel as though you'd bought yourself a gift. Many stores have specific ways of handling the transaction as well. Nordstrom clerks will never hand you the bag over the cash register like a sack of potatoes. They carefully pack it for you, finish the transaction, and then walk around the counter to hand your bag to you in a poised and civilized way, no matter how busy the store is that day. And many high-end men's stores have a very particular way they show merchandise to customers, gracefully draping the tie over their arm to show you what it looks like instead of holding it up like a dangling wet fish.

These little touches all make sense in the context of the larger Brand Strategy. Once your strategy is clear, you can find a thousand creative ways to parlay that brand into each and every customer interaction.

> Once your strategy is clear, you can find a thousand creative ways to parlay that brand into each and every customer interaction.

And you won't be performing random acts—they will all fit together within the brand promise. This is the little secret that will truly delight your customers.

Many companies with good products or services haven't succeeded in business, but the ones that use brand to surprise and enchant their customers at every turn often create rabid fans.

Virgin America Airlines does this very well, conveying their fun, hip, and laid-back style in every detail: soft pink or purple in-cabin lighting; TVs at every seat where you can order food at any time; cleverly worded, slightly irreverent gate signage, such as, "While impressive, if your bag is bigger than 24 inches x 16 inches x 10 inches, it must be checked"; and even their original in-flight safety video. Rather than a stiff actor giving me the same instructions we've started to tune out on every other flight, Virgin America shows a stylized animated video with all sorts of crazy characters— even a bull calmly reading a magazine next to an anxious bullfighter. The company's sassy, humorous tone carries over to the script as well: "For the 0.0001 percent of you who've never operated a seat belt before, here's how it works."

Virgin America has recently updated their safety video and has outdone itself again. Flyers are now treated to a sleek, choreographed hip-hop number that offers several dance styles, including animation, b-boy, break dancing, Broadway, contemporary, contortion, finger-tutting, jazz, lyrical, pop-and-locking, tango, and waving. Delightful surprises include a groovy nun, robotic dancers demonstrating the life vest and even a child rapper.[16] It's such a simple thing but is indeed another customer touchpoint they chose to use as a brand opportunity. After all, they want to make flying fun again.

> Small businesses have these same opportunities to be creative, regardless of budget.

Small businesses have these same opportunities to be creative, regardless of budget. Look for those opportunities, however small, and find ways to seal your brand onto the heart of your customers. Best of all, many touches don't need to cost you an additional dime if you can get creative with things you already provide, as we'll see from Red Dingo's story below.

Brand at Work: Red Dingo

Little things do mean a lot—even wording your customer thank-you note in an innovative way. Red Dingo (Reddingo.com) designs and markets pet accessories. That's what they do. What they *are* is a young, progressive company that believes "near enough isn't good enough." When I ordered my black lab Eddie's new ID tag, it came in the mail with a card—addressed to Eddie—saying they hoped he enjoyed his new tag, and it would help him find his way back home from all his adventures. They knew that I as a customer cared about my pet, or I wouldn't have ordered this stylish little ID tag. I mean, Eddie didn't pick it out himself. They knew I'd get a kick out of having the card addressed to my dog. It also made me feel like they see my pet as I do: a member of the family. Having a warm, playful brand affected their decisions right down to how my order was packaged and worded. A regular *"Thank you for your order"* would have been acceptable, but that wasn't good enough for them.

Hire Well: Every New Hire Is a Brand Ambassador

I once worked for a large, multinational software company. We had a strong vision and good corporate values and it was a great place to work. But I never quite felt the company's vision and values actually connected to what we did on a daily basis. Many companies face this challenge to apply their guiding principles on a practical level. I didn't think we had a well-defined brand, though all the pieces were there, ripe for a full-blown brand execution. We were well-respected, trustworthy, and our customers loved us.

Then, new marketing leaders came in and tried to move the brand a few steps in the right direction. The advertising became more inspirational, showing people how our software could help them do their jobs better, instead of rattling off a list of features and functions (as every other B2B software company seems to do). And while this was definitely the right direction, I always felt it wasn't grounded in anything real. The claims weren't grounded in a larger corporate Brand Strategy. Everything came from the marketing department, and we weren't embracing the brand holistically as a company, deep down in our bones. What was finance's role to play in that customer promise? Or engineering? Or even legal?

Then one day I saw an intriguing email go out. It was an internal HTML email from human resources, showcasing all the recruiting sites and activities that their team had implemented. I clicked around on some of these sites meant for outside recruits. They talked about sports teams the company sponsored, community events we supported, and the like. I was floored by the information. First of all, as an employee I didn't know half the things we were sponsoring as a company, yet HR was promoting these activities to people who didn't even work there! I was on the grant committee and knew about our own office's amazing community activities but not the work from our other global offices. This was all being presented to potential new hires as part of our brand. But I *worked* for the company and didn't even know this was our brand and what we were portraying ourselves to be. It was actually kind of cool: I remember saying, "Wow! This is a company I would totally work for!"

Now, as I said, this was indeed a great company for which to work, but my issue was the fact that HR presented a brand to potential new hires that wasn't quite the reality of working there. And I knew this because I worked there and had experienced none of these things. I thought it was kind of sad that HR had developed a clearer brand for the company than its own marketing team. What amazing things could we have achieved if marketing and HR had been in lockstep on messaging? We could have been attracting more of the right customers and employees to truly live that brand inside and out.

Indeed, brand can be a huge recruitment tool for a company, as was the case with Bakery on Main. In the following Brand at Work case study, the company did a great job of recreating a local bakery experience online, and that strong brand enticed one of their most loyal customer fans to actually seek work at the company.

Brand at Work: Bakery on Main

Many people love the smells and sights of their local neighborhood bakery. But that experience is different if you have celiac disease and need to eat gluten-free products that often taste bland and boring. In 2003, Michael Smulders launched Bakery on Main (Bakeryonmain.com) from the back of his natural foods store to provide tasty, gluten-free granola. People loved it and the company now distributes its delicious products internationally and online. Their mission is to make foods that are good for you but taste like they aren't. While the present focus is on gluten-free granola, they purposefully crafted a company name, logo, and mission to more generally refer to great-tasting natural products of any kind, so the brand can extend to more products in the future.

Trying to capture that small-bakery feel, the brand focuses on being homegrown, tasty, casual, local, neighborly, and trustworthy, and only delivering quality products. Even though you can't walk into their store when you buy over the web, the company recently revamped their website with a homey feel to create an online experience that makes you feel like you've walked into the bakery. The striped awnings in their logo and on their new packaging convey a neighborhood feeling, and this consistency creates an instant connection.

The brand attribute of "quality" is proven through their Kosher Parve designation and both their non-GMO and gluten-free certifications. They also only partner with the best suppliers that meet a rigorous selection process to show they adhere to strict manufacturing and ingredient standards. This further builds consumer trust. The "trustworthy" brand attribute comes out on their website, which includes transparent and detailed product ingredient information, full production disclosure, and facts about the facility.

Perhaps the best brand compliment? Their marketing manager, Sara Lefebvre, was a loyal customer and jumped at the chance to work there. "I was attracted to their story and their humble beginnings, not to mention the great taste. As someone with celiac disease, I can identify with our customers and have a unique passion for the company."

I'm amazed more businesses don't link up their marketing and HR teams and have them work together. Both groups are responsible for vital internal and external communications that should be aligned. The marketing department can spearhead brand-building efforts but they don't own brand evangelism: that's everyone's job.

If hiring practices are closely aligned with brand efforts, then the HR team can make better hiring decisions and attract the right kind of people, who will in turn embrace and live out the brand, thus further cementing it externally. And the cycle will continue. But if you don't know your brand well, you can't possibly determine if people will be a good fit for your organization or if their values align with yours. Brand can provide a litmus test to not only communicate the right things about your company to customers, but also to potential employees—and even partners.

> The marketing department can spearhead brand-building efforts but they don't *own* brand evangelism: that's everyone's job.

If I'd followed my own advice, I'd have seen a red flag waving a mile away when I interviewed with a technology start-up firm years ago. In my interview with the product marketing manager, I asked, "What kind of culture would you say you have here?"

His answer was, "We don't have a culture, but that's why we need a strong marketing director. Marketing can create one for us."

Wow. I should have run away right then and there. Marketing can craft and shepherd the right brand, based on market demand, competitive analysis, and customer feedback. It's their job to take all of that information, synthesize it, and then figure out the best way to convey the right image and messages to the world in order to attract more sales and customers. And yes, it can even inform internal processes and policies if there is executive sponsorship from the top.

But marketing cannot bear the sole responsibility of forcing a culture or brand on a company. If, as I've said throughout this book, brand is part of every activity and interaction, then every employee has a role to play in fulfilling that brand promise. So they have to know what it is, embrace it, understand it, and contribute to it. I believe great brand adoption starts at the top and rolls downhill. If the founder or CEO commits to a strong brand vision, verbalized and perfected by the marketing team in many cases, the rest of the company will fall in line. But if the person at the top doesn't think brand is important and isn't creating a mission-based organization, then the true assets of that organization—the people—will reflect that attitude as well.

Josh Levine of Great Monday (Great-monday.com), a business consultancy that builds brands from the inside out, calls this *culture-driven branding*. "Programs that have the most effect are the ones that engage people within the company. It's all about culture—the sum of the decisions that any one person or group makes," says Josh.

How do you engage your people to understand and make better decisions about what they're doing day in and day out? Josh says if you can teach your employees the company values, they will make better decisions on how that brand is expressed in their jobs. "Your people are making decisions time and time again, and a company's money will be much better spent if it's able to create and invest in a brand-education program that propagates itself." If your people know why they are coming to work, they can align to your mission and help you achieve it. Give them a purpose and control over their destiny.

That's the amazing opportunity available to entrepreneurs, small business CEOs, and startup firms. You are young and you are nimble. You're closer to your customers and employees than large corporations. You have the power to create a brand as amazingly sticky as Apple, Nike, or Virgin if you want. But your Brand Strategy needs to start at the top and permeate not just advertising and marketing, but hiring, operations, customer care, finance, production, and every other aspect of your company. It can help determine the right people to bring into the organization and ensure they'll be ambassadors for your brand.

When to Rebrand

Rebranding can mean overhauling your visual look and feel, or simply updating your messaging to adapt to changing needs, different competitors, a new market, or customer feedback. It means you're making a new promise to your target audience and you need to reposition that difference in everything you do. We may only take notice of visual rebranding efforts because they're most apparent. But brands can and should evolve, even if their core mission remains the same. Most companies will stay true at their core to the mission-based brand promise they offer, in terms of their operations, product quality, and ideal customer, but they try to update their look, tweak their messaging, or change distribution strategies to adapt to changing tastes and needs.

My favorite example of this is a story from Guy Kawasaki's book, *Rules for Revolutionaries* (Harper Collins). His story wasn't framed in the context of rebranding, but it's a great example of retooling your message to fit market needs. In 1886, a woman named Josephine Cochrane invented the dishwasher. She didn't do this to save time and effort, as she had many servants who performed these tasks for her. But her servants broke too many dishes cleaning them manually so she invented the dishwasher to save her china. This helped her sell her product to hotels and restaurants—but not to homeowners. Why? Homeowners didn't consider washing dishes a hard task. So she tweaked her message to focus on the dishwasher's ability to sterilize the dishes in extremely hot water and keep your family healthier. The brand's benefit for that audience was changed to focus on better health rather than saving time.

While you don't want to change your brand every six months, some reasons to rebrand could include:

- Your colors and imagery are dated (e.g., you will be viewed as behind the times and irrelevant)

- You are now targeting a different buyer (e.g., you used to sell only to women and now want to attract more men; you used to sell to low-level analysts and you now sell to C-level execs)

- Your offerings or price points have changed (e.g., from a cheap technology tool to an expensive solution suite)

- You have direct feedback that your brand is repelling your target customer or is being completely misinterpreted (e.g., suffering through a string of bad press or damaging misinformation about your product or service quality

• Your competition has changed (e.g., more competitors
  have swarmed the market and all of you look and
  sound the same)

Another big reason companies rebrand is due to a merger,
acquisition, or change in positioning. Monster.com was a client
of mine when I worked for Young & Laramore, a midwestern ad
agency, back in 1999. That year, the Monster Board (as it was known)
merged with our client, Online Career Center (OCC), because
OCC was well-known and respected among HR professionals—the
ones paying for the ads. This was a symbiotic deal. The combined
company rebranded as Monster.com and revamped their look,
feel, and messaging in advance of the big launch.

At the same time, Monster.com needed to relaunch within the
Human Resources (HR) community to tout that OCC was now
Monster.com and offered new, advanced online features. More
importantly, Monster.com needed to reposition the brand in the
eyes of HR professionals, who still thought of the old Monster
Board brand as one that only attracted young, inexperienced job
seekers, or worse, those who couldn't find a job anywhere else.
Old brand perceptions die hard: Monster.com had to shift those
mental perceptions—not just change their look and feel.

At the time, online job boards were new and Internet usage
wasn't as pervasive as it is today. Many recruiters were still spending
money on newspaper classified ads and not investing heavily online.
So the brand positioning had to compete with not only other online
job boards but with traditional media options.

The old company put heavy emphasis on résumé *quantity*
instead on *quality*. Their name—The Monster Board—emphasized
huge numbers of résumés, not quality candidates. No one had more
résumés or job seekers, their positioning screamed. All of their
benefits focused on "more, more, more." Now, with this newly
combined company, Monster.com had to create a different brand

position to entice both job seekers and recruiters while addressing each of their unique needs.

While our agency dealt with the HR positioning, we saw how both the recruiter and the job seeker positioning were inextricably linked: If you didn't feed the engine with qualified candidates, then you wouldn't attract more recruiters. And if you didn't have good recruiters posting on the site, you'd never attract high-caliber job seekers. The promises to each audience had to be delivered at the same time.

After interviews and focus groups with HR managers, we found the online benefit of quantity was important, but it also produced a new need: filtering résumés. Soon, *quality* trumped *quantity*. Recruiters were less concerned with seeing hundreds of résumés than they were with finding one *perfect* résumé. There was one job to fill and only one person needed to fill it. The rest was just clutter. (This was in the day before niche and industry-specific job-posting sites, which solved many of these problems.) So we focused the positioning on quality, not quantity. Yes, it was true that with more "crop" you tend to find more "cream" (one of our ad headlines) but that assumed there was quality in that crop to begin with.

A recruiter always loves to find someone *before* they're starting a job search. The brand positioning shifted to convince HR execs that Monster.com didn't attract the desperately unemployed, but attracted those who were currently employed and might be open to a better opportunity. After all, everyone in any job has a bad day or dreams of career improvement. These more desirable candidates weren't actively looking but could be convinced it was safe to look. We called these people "the vaguely dissatisfied." In this way, recruiters could get in front of quality candidates and find the perfect one.

On the other side of the funnel, the job-seeker messaging focused on quality as well—quality as it pertained to finding the perfect job. Monster.com wasn't about having the most jobs, but about finding a job that fit your aspirations and passions. That message was captured in the company's famous "When I Grow Up" 1999 Super Bowl ad, created by Monster.com's consumer ad agency, Mullen. The humorous black-and-white ad featured a series of hopeful children saying things like, "When I grow up, I want to . . . be a yes-man," and ". . . have a brown nose" and ". . . be forced into early retirement." The message wasn't merely, "Find a job at Monster.com" but "Find a *better* job at Monster.com."

This quality-of-life messaging worked to get more job seekers onto the site, which satisfied the needs of all those new recruiters we were attracting through print and online ads. Job searches per minute, a crucial measurement for Monster.com, spiked post-Super Bowl and remained high for days afterward.[17]

In another example, my firm Red Slice worked with Talent Technology to help them rebrand both visually and verbally. Talent Technology is a Canadian-based firm and was primarily known as an HR technology tool provider targeted to IT professionals. With a new product suite, they aimed to sell a higher-priced strategic business solution and have more conversations with higher level C-suite executives, such as the CEO and CFO, which required a different message, value proposition—and yes, look and feel. They launched a new product-solution suite which we named Talemetry to help companies source and engage a qualified talent pool. This positioning shift was so successful in attracting and engaging their target audience, they actually rebranded the entire company as Talemetry (Talemetry.com)!

Often a company may need to rebrand—or create an entirely new brand—when they find a new use for their products or a new audience that demands what they offer. Such was the case when the Edward Mirell brand spun off from its parent company to carve out an entirely new market which it could lead.

\\

Brand at Work: Edward Mirell

How can you grow a brand to serve a completely different market? When your market is crowded, you often have to forge a new category that plays to your strengths so you can be heard above the crowd. High-end jewelry design brand Edward Mirell (Edwardmirell.com) leveraged its experience in innovative design, manufacturing, and marketing to establish itself as the recognized leader of a new jewelry category.

Edward Mirell's parent company is Spectore Corporation, which spent years of research in titanium development with a singular focus on titanium's applications for consumer products. "As our pallet of materials and technologies grew, so did the number of inquiries and orders from many of the world's leading brands. In 2004 we decided it was time for us to apply our vast and uniquely diverse resources in design, development, and manufacturing expertise into a signature brand: Edward Mirell," says Edward Rosenberg, designer and CEO. Edward Mirell is a privately held, design-jewelry brand focused on using contemporary metals, like titanium, and cutting-edge technology to break new ground in fashion.

Their brand oozes boldness, edginess, innovation, and exceptional quality. You can see this in their website: a modern, elegant look of bold blacks and grays. Their copy expertly uses all the right words to craft their story. The tone is aspirational, epic, and carries exactly the right sense of high-end "coolness"—minus any pretension.

By their very nature, these products appeal to people who want something different—and diversity is key to the brand's success. "We recognize that our lofty goal involves clearly defining difference at every turn," says Rosenberg. "So we approach every initiative by exploring the broadest possible diversity in design, process, display, and marketing. For example, only a small percentage of the design and development teams in our jewelry division come from the jewelry world. We have graphic designers, animators, illustrators, sculptors, fashion designers, engineers, architects, and industrial designers all working together. Vive la différence."

The company knows a differentiated brand cannot be successful if it tries to please everyone. Their jewelry pieces tend to appeal to tech communities and alternative-lifestyle groups. Edward Mirell's target consumers are fashion-forward and career-driven with a passion for excitement and travel. Typical of generations X and Y, they follow the latest trends and are brand-conscious while seeking value and quality in the items they purchase. They are educated; therefore, they research and understand style innovations, the latest materials and intricacies, or quality in design. The proof is in numerous design awards, world-renowned partner organizations, a loyal fan base, and many celebrity devotees.

In line with their unique and cutting-edge brand, Edward Mirell continues to invent, develop, and introduce unique new technologies to stand out in the marketplace. In 2013, it introduced new collections that use the most advanced bonding and forming technologies to integrate precious and contemporary materials that marry art and science in ways never before imagined. Named "More Than One," these new design achievements marry century old traditions of jewelry materials and craftsmanship to today's most advanced strategic materials and technologies. Why the name "More Than One?" The answer is simple; the future is infinite.

You can see there's an important time and place for rebranding, but this doesn't mean you should do it all the time. It is easy to get scared and second-guess yourself with branding as you see more innovative and creative options out there. If you consistently communicate a clear brand and you know you're tapping into the right needs for your audience, then you shouldn't worry. Good designers keep changing styles in mind when creating your visual identity. They should avoid colors or designs that are too trendy and become outdated in a year.

However, if your brand is about being on the cutting edge and being modern, this can be a fine line to walk. You should be able to maintain whatever you select for at least a few years, not only to keep your costs down in changing everything out, but to ensure the brand gains momentum with people. While you may be sick of your branding after six months, many of your ideal customers will only have interacted with it once or twice. They haven't had a chance to form a connection yet. Nike started using the swoosh graphic many years ago and now it's come to symbolize their brand promise, given the amount of time and money they've put into it. The company's brand promise has evolved over time, but it remains true to the core of what they deliver. That has never changed.

You may find you eventually need to update the look and feel of your brand to stand out from what is now a crowded marketplace or to inject new life into the brand. Rebranding can be a great way to build buzz again and shake up customer apathy. But be careful how you do this.

Scott Montgomery, the executive creative director and principal for brand innovation firm Bradley and Montgomery (bamideas. com), from whom we heard in Part 1 of the book, states, "Updating branding is one of the precious few controls a marketer has to create energy and news around an established brand. But it has to be more than just a logical, clever, and systematic undertaking. Will change enhance the story the brand embodies without losing sight of its history?"

Intimately understanding your Brand Strategy—your core reason for being—and staying tuned to why customers buy from you at both a conscious and subconscious level can help you avoid slip-ups when it comes time to update your look.

Get to Know Your Customers—Intimately

Earlier, we talked about the single most important aspect of your brand: knowing your ideal customer or client. This is not something you do once and then you're done: You must constantly be talking with them, reassessing their needs, and ensuring your brand resonates with them. The more you learn about them, the more you can refine your brand to speak directly to them.

As we just mentioned, one big reason companies rebrand is to target a new ideal customer. In the beginning, you had to start somewhere and make an informed decision about who your brand will target and what they want. But as you work with your clients and customers, you will have an instant focus group and a wealth of information at your fingertips. It's amazing how often organizations don't just ask their clients, customers, or donors what they want, why they buy, what they need, or whether the brand is on the right path.

Mike Michalowicz, marketing consultant, author, and speaker from whom we heard earlier, advises you to collect customer information face to face if possible. "You've got to see them in their own environment, otherwise they won't trust you. Help them be comfortable so they will speak from the heart. You've got to see the makeup of people. You've got to live with your customer." Not only does he attend live conferences to constantly connect with his customers, but he has literally moved in with them! "I've rented a cabin in Denver and invited my top consulting clients for retreats," says Mike. "For four days, we cook, play cards, talk shop. This helps me understand my customers as family and get inside their minds."

Mike shares a great example of targeting the wrong audience. When he first published *The Toilet Paper Entrepreneur,* he could not seem to find the book anywhere. "While we initially thought the book's ideal audience was college students, our target audience ended up being women re-entering the workforce and creating their own businesses, who were much older, about forty-five or fifty years old!" Once he realized this, he constantly interviewed them about their business plans, hopes, and dreams. He stumbled upon trust as an important emotion they needed to feel from his brand. In getting to know them intimately and hearing their personal stories, Mike found out that many of these women had male figures in their lives—husbands, fathers, teachers—who did not support their endeavors and, in some cases, verbally abused them. In turn, the women developed a distrust for male authority figures (like Mike) advising them on what they should do. So he simply asked them, "What establishes trust?" These conversations led to incremental brand-positioning insights: He always keeps his wedding ring on in photos. He takes out any potential "creepy" factor by flaunting his average, regular-guy, authentic self, often sharing goofy videos and funny (but powerful) content. All of this makes him more trustworthy and approachable than many other male business gurus out there.

Talk to your customers. Seek out your desired audience where they gather, such as conferences, association meetings, or clubs and engage them in conversation. Send them an online survey or, better yet, host a wine-and-cheese reception to ask them about what they need, value, or despise as it relates to what you offer. You don't need to pay thousands for fancy focus groups or research projects to ensure your brand in on track. Just reach out and ask.

Everything Stems From Brand

The right Brand Strategy is the core to building a strong organization. The brand may indeed evolve over time, but it's important to think about your reason for being, your ideal customers, and your corporate personality before you embark on building a website, a logo, or any of the other visual representations of brand. Consult your brand before you create corporate messaging or put any marketing programs in place. Otherwise, you'll waste time and money and not grow your business at all.

Your Brand Strategy serves as the guidepost to all your business decisions, ranging from which marketing tactics to employ to how to decorate your store to what colors and font to use on your website to the type of people you hire. If you can't believe in and articulate your brand, then no one else will. Brand can inform your operations inside and out to give customers a more consistent experience. And while your brand ultimately lives in the minds of customers, you can influence those perceptions and attitudes with many tools that are within your control.

A Brand Strategy will give you a host of benefits as you move forward. You'll be able to define who you are and who you serve, crisply and cleanly. You can more efficiently spread the word about what you do by pairing the right messages with the right tactics. You will focus on only the most effective channels to reach your target audience. You can tailor messaging for different audiences that still contains a unified mission and vision. And tactically, you'll save time and money on design, writing, and promotion.

> You might be small, but you can think big.

You might be small, but you can think big. Use brand as the opportunity to create a mission-driven organization that adds something to the world and to the lives of those you touch: customers, employees, partners, and even the community at large. Who knows? Maybe someday, a loyal customer, client or supporter will tattoo *your* logo onto their arm with pride.

Recommended Reading List

Looking for more inspiration to clarify your brand, craft compelling content, and get your creative juices flowing? Enjoy this reading list cultivated by both me and the experts featured throughout *Branding Basics for Small Business*. May these spark your creativity, sharpen your savvy, and improve your communication as you build an irresistible brand!

The Art of Communicating by Thich Nhat Hanh (HarperOne). Written by a Buddhist monk, this book teaches you how to be compassionate through language. The author offers a great model for how to build a big empire but still remain mindful and compassionate.

Bird by Bird: Some Instructions on Writing and Life by Anne Lamott (Anchor). A wise and witty read on the reality of the writer's life and how to find your true voice and passion when weaving words.

Book Yourself Solid: The Fastest, Easiest, and Most Reliable System for Getting More Clients Than You Can Handle Even if You Hate Marketing and Selling by Michael Port (Wiley). A business development and promotional guide for service businesses that want more brand awareness and clients.

The Brand Gap: How to Bridge the Distance Between Business Strategy and Design by Marty Neumeier (New Riders). Deceptively simple yet powerfully insightful, this book is an entertaining and fast read to help organizations bridge the gap between brand strategy and customer experience. Neumeier lays out five disciplines to turn brand theory into an organization's reality—and offers new perspectives to even the most experienced brand marketers.

Content Rules: How to Create Killer Blogs, Podcasts, Videos, Ebooks (and More) That Engage Customers and Ignite Your Business by Ann Handley and C.C. Chapman (Wiley). With the onslaught of new social media platforms giving everyone a "voice"—including organizations and their customers—good content is vital to online success. This book blends art and science to show you step by step how to create content that people care about so you can engage fans, generate demand, and ignite your business. It includes many case studies of how companies have successfully spread their ideas online.

David and Goliath: Underdogs, Misfits, and the Art of Battling Giants by Malcolm Gladwell (Little, Brown and Company). Citing classic tales and history, Gladwell shows how scrappy underdogs can use their status to their advantage. Quite an inspiration for a small organization facing stiff competition from larger guys with deeper pockets!

Decisive: How to Make Better Choices in Life and Work by Chip Heath and Dan Heath (Crown Business). A fascinating read about the drivers behind how people and organizations make decisions, and how to overcome underlying biases and habits so that better choices can lead to more success.

Different: Escaping the Competitive Herd by Youngme Moon (Crown Business). A Harvard Business School professor, Moon has written an easy-to-read, conversational book that advises organizations to resist "what everyone else is doing" and instead offer something that is meaningfully different. Numerous case studies highlight mavericks and innovators who have staked out bold, adventurous positions—and won the hearts and minds of their target audience.

Drive: The Surprising Truth about What Motivates Us by Daniel Pink (Riverhead Books). A must-read book about effectively managing teams and influencing customers. Drawing on four decades of scientific research on human motivation, Pink exposes the mismatch between what science knows and what business does—and how that affects every aspect of life.

I'm at a Networking Event—Now What???: A Guide to Getting the Most Out of Any Networking Event by Sandy Jones-Kaminski (Happy About). Everything you need to know about mastering the art of building your brand and connecting with others at networking events—even if you're the most extreme introvert.

Jab, Jab, Jab, Right Hook: How to Tell Your Story in a Noisy Social World by Gary Vaynerchuk (HarperBusiness). This book offers a blueprint for social media strategies that work so you can connect with customers and beat the competition. Recommended for advice that is easy to implement.

Made to Stick: Why Some Ideas Survive and Others Die by Chip Heath and Dan Heath (Random House). Learn the traits of "sticky messages" and how to get your big ideas to be remembered, acted upon, and shared.

The New Rules of Marketing & PR: How to Use Social Media, Online Video, Mobile Applications, Blogs, News Releases, and Viral Marketing to Reach Buyers Directly by David Meerman Scott (Wiley). This book offers a step-by-step action plan for using modern marketing and PR tactics to connect with buyers, increase brand awareness, and generate sales. It details how organizations of all sizes can leverage web-based content to get the right information to the right people at the right time for a fraction of the cost of big-budget campaigns.

Propel: Five Ways to Amp Up Your Marketing and Accelerate Business by Whitney Keyes (Career Press). Blending traditional marketing techniques and social media tools, this book covers five nimble marketing strategies to help organizations of any size quickly capture market share, customers, and brand awareness.

The Pumpkin Plan: A Simple Strategy to Grow a Remarkable Business in Any Field by Mike Michalowicz (Portfolio Hardcover). This book is full of unconventional strategies to build a profitable company. Michalowicz's practical advice and witty humor make this a fun read.

Purple Cow, New Edition: Transform Your Business by Being Remarkable by Seth Godin (Portfolio Hardcover). A manifesto for marketers to always strive to create something noticeable, extraordinary, and exciting so your organization can stand out from the crowd and win.

Reinventing You: Define Your Brand, Imagine Your Future by Dorie Clark (Harvard Business Review Press). While focused more on building a personal brand, this book provides great step-by-step advice you can apply to building an authentic and compelling brand online in the modern age of social media.

Switch: How to Change Things When Change Is Hard by
Chip Heath and Dan Heath (Crown Business). An excellent read
on clever ways that even the smallest organizations and least
influential people can impact change and drive behavior. Digs into
the psychology of the rational mind and the emotional mind—and
how to speak to both.

**The Toilet Paper Entrepreneur: The Tell-It-Like-It-Is Guide to
Cleaning Up in Business, Even If You Are at the End of Your
Roll** by Mike Michalowicz (Obsidian Launch, LLC). Blending
solid advice, real-world case studies, and lots of humor, this book
inspires entrepreneurs with great ideas and little resources to
create the business of their dreams.

Youtility: Why Smart Marketing Is about Help Not Hype by
Jay Baer (Portfolio Hardcover). A smart look at how "selling" has
changed in today's overhyped marketing world, and how brands
that aim to first provide value and truly connect with customers
will win.

Zag: The Number One Strategy of High-Performance Brands
by Marty Neumeier (New Riders). This book drills deep into
how brands can harness the power of differentiation: when other
organizations zig, you must zag. Neumeier presents a powerful
case for why traditional differentiation is no longer enough—
today, companies need radical differentiation to create lasting
value. The author's "whiteboard" visual-layout style makes this
easy to read in one sitting, yet the insights will remain with you
long after.

About the Author

Maria Ross is a brand strategist, author and speaker who believes cash flow and creativity are not mutually exclusive. As founder of Red Slice, she advises start-ups, entrepreneurs and small to midsize growth businesses on how to translate captivating stories into irresistible brands. Maria is the author of *Branding Basics for Small Business* and her humorous and heartfelt memoir *Rebooting My Brain*. A dynamic speaker on both business and inspirational topics, she delights audiences ranging from *The New York Times* to the Chamber of Commerce to BlogHer with her wit and wisdom and has appeared in numerous media outlets, including MSNBC, ABC News, The Huffington Post, Forbes.com, NPR and Entrepreneur Magazine. Maria lives in the San Francisco Bay Area with her husband Paul, their precocious black lab Eddie and a new son on the way.

For wise perspectives and winsome wit, please visit Maria's blog at Red-slice.com and sign up for her email list. You can also contact and learn more from Maria by joining her Twitter battalion @RedSlice or becoming a fan at Facebook.com/RedSlice.

Acknowledgements

So many people contribute to the birth of a book. And yet only the author's name goes on the cover! Thank goodness for acknowledgments.

Thanks to Dee and Sammie Justesen and Nadene Carter at NorlightsPress for making this book a reality and encouraging me to update to this latest edition.

As mentioned in the first edition, I wouldn't be writing today without the support of my amazing family. Thanks to the Piccininni family who has encouraged (or patiently tolerated?) my writing, musings, and opinions since the tender age of five. And thanks to the DeMauro and Ross families for their cheerleading.

Thanks to my original writing support group of Whitney Keyes and Elisabeth Dale for making this book possible. For research, thanks to Carlie Hanson for her help with the first edition and Andy Lo for his help with the most recent one. And thanks again to Sarah Wilson, Outspoken Media, Karen Rosenzweig, Betsy Talbot, Emilia Skrinar, and Lucia Carruthers for helping with publicity on the first edition.

This recent edition would not have been possible without the generosity of all the experts quoted throughout the book, especially those who helped add fresh content and perspective. Thank you for your time and for trusting me with your words. You are wonderful teachers.

And a big thank you to Lori Zue for her deft and detailed editing on this recent edition. Thank heaven for your eagle eyes!

Many mentors have contributed—whether they know it or not—to my branding philosophies and education. I thank them from the bottom of my inquisitive heart.

Thanks to Scott Montgomery and Mark Bradley for the wonderful branding work they create and for balancing artistic integrity with business reality (very rare indeed). Years ago, you welcomed me over from the "big, bad Account Management side" of our ad agency and patiently answered my every question as I sought to learn more about the magic you do. Thanks to Carrie Voorhis, a gifted writer who teaches me about the power of words to move people; to Marty Neumeier, a brand guru I admire for his brilliant simplicity; and to Kathi Kaplan, Caroline Waterson, and Susan Marfise who taught me the power of marketing planning and how "fewer activities done the right way" will yield greater success. Thanks to Patrick Morrissey, Guy Weismantel, and Lance Walter— master storytellers who bring brand personality to an often bland industry; to Melody Biringer, entrepreneur extraordinaire, for being a constant inspiration and good friend; to Bridget Perez, Isabelle Englund-Geiger, and Scott Lawrence for their tremendous design and digital abilities grounded in brand truths. Special thanks to Bridget for this book's cover design.

Thank you to my big brand heroes like Nike, Apple, Starbucks, and Virgin for having the courage to connect on an emotional level with your customers. I learn more from you all the time. Big thanks to the amazing small businesses profiled in the book who trusted me with an inside look, and to my beloved Red Slice clients. Your desire to create something meaningful in the world inspires me no end.

Most importantly, thanks to Paul, my husband and friend, who not only constantly teaches me about product marketing and messaging, but who adores me, encourages me, and paves the way to making everything possible while supporting all my crazy ideas. Love you.

End Notes

1. Ashley Koehn, "The Power of Team," http://inside.nike. com/blogs/nikewomenen_US/2009/04/27/the-power-of-team (April 27, 2009)

2. *CorpComms Magazine*, "Making London Hip Again," www. corp commsmagazine.co.uk, (October 6, 2009)

3. *National Textile Center: Annual Report*, "The Pivotal Role of Brand Image in Purchase Decisions," (October 2009)

4. BrandZ, *Top 100 Most Valuable Global Brands Report 2012*, www.brandz.com (2012)

5. Linda Tischler, "Never Mind! Pepsi Pulls Much-loathed Tropicana Packaging," http://www.FastCompany.com (February 23, 2009)

6. Monica Langley, *The Wall Street Journal*, "Clinton, Bush Advisors Steeped in Crisis Join Forces," (July 9, 2008)

7. Maria Ross, *Red Slice,* "Using social media to delight and provoke, plus how studios know whether to cast Ashton or not" http://red-slice.com/2010/01/ask-the-expert-using-social-media-to-delight-provoke-plus-how-studios-know-whether-to-cast-ashton-or-not/ (January 7, 2010)

8. Press release, "FY 14 First Quarter Results Conference Call" http://www.apple.com/pr/library/2014/01/23FY-14-First-Quarter-Results-Conference-Call.html

9. Jeffrey McCracken and Peter Lattman, *The Wall Street Journal*, "Sharper Image Lives—As a Brand," (June 26, 2008)

10. Noreen O'Leary, *Brandweek*, "Report: Starbucks, Wells Fargo Surge in Customer Loyalty," (January 30, 2010)

11. Joseph B. White, *The Wall Street Journal*, "Dude, Where's My Car?" (October 28, 2009)

12. Shortly before going to print. Intersource unexpectedly lost its founder and visionary Jack Leary. Condolences to his family, friends, colleagues and staff who had the good fortune of knowing him. He is dearly missed.

13. Criteria listed with author permission from *The Brand Gap: How to Bridge the Distance Between Business Strategy and Design* (New Riders Press)

14. Press release, "Theo Chocolate Expands Distribution to Canada" www.theochocolate.com/news/press-release/theo-chocolate-expands-distribution-canada

15. Allie Townsend, "2013 Year in Review: Top Global Life Events" http://www.facebookstories.com/2013/en-en/top-life-events (December 9, 2013)

16. Kate Goodman, "The Virgin America Safety Dance... in Numbers" http://www.virgin.com/news/the-virgin-america-safety-dance%E2%80%A6-in-numbers (November 1, 2013)

17. Paul McNamara, "Monster.com's Super Bowl Ads Pay Off in a Big Way," http://www.cnn.com (February 8, 1999)

Made in the USA
Middletown, DE
24 November 2015